68000 Microprocessor
Handbook

68000 Microprocessor Handbook

Gerry Kane

OSBORNE/McGraw-Hill
Berkeley, California

This book may be used to update *An Introduction to Microcomputers: Volume 2 — Some Real Microprocessors,* Osborne/McGraw-Hill, 1978.

Published by
OSBORNE/McGraw-Hill
630 Bancroft Way
Berkeley, California 94710
U.S.A.

For information on translations and book distributors outside of the U. S. A., please write OSBORNE/McGraw-Hill at the above address.

68000 MICROPROCESSOR HANDBOOK

Copyright © 1981 McGraw-Hill, Inc. All rights reserved. Printed in the United States of America. No part of this publication may be reproduced, stored in a retrieval system, or transmitted in any form or by any means, electronic, mechanical, photocopying, recording or otherwise without the prior written permission of the publishers.

234567890   CPCP 898765432

ISBN 0-931988-41-1

Technical edit by Lyle Graham

Cover design by Marc Miyashiro

Contents

1
Introduction

The MC68000 microprocessor is Motorola's first 16-bit microprocessor. It is the third of the new generation of these devices, having been preceded by Intel's 8086 and Zilog's Z8000. Detailed descriptions of the 8086 and Z8000 microprocessors are provided in the *OSBORNE 16-Bit Microprocessor Handbook*, OSBORNE/McGraw-Hill, 1981.

The MC68000 is not program compatible with Motorola's family of 8-bit microprocessors. Motorola has opted for designing an instruction set which provides maximum power and simplicity rather than compatibility.

MC68000 Features Versus 8086/Z8000

The following is a discussion of interesting MC68000 features as compared to similar capabilities of the Z8000 and 8086:

1. The MC68000 overlaps the fetching of each instruction's object code with the decoding and execution at the two prior instructions to obtain a pipeline effect. The Z8000 uses this approach, but only under certain circumstances. On the other hand, the 8086 performs extensive pipelining using a 6-byte object code pipeline.

2. Both the 8086 and the Z8000 family of microprocessors provide methods of operating the devices in a "simple" system configuration or "complex" system configuration. The 8086 accomplishes this within a single device by having a number of dual-function pins which serve one function in simple systems and another function in complex systems. The Z8000, on the other hand, is supplied in two versions: the Z8001 for complex configurations and the Z8002 for simple configurations. The MC68000 is contained in a 64-pin package and therefore need not attempt to accommodate different complexities of system configurations; it is always capable of operating in what is effectively a "maximum" or "complex" system configuration mode.

3. The MC68000 has built-in logic to handle bus access arbitration in

multi-CPU configurations. The 8086 and the Z8000 have equivalent logic.

4. The MC68000 can directly access up to 16 million (16M) bytes of memory with its 24-bit Address Bus. This memory space may be expanded to 64M bytes by using the Function Code lines. In comparison, the 8086 can directly address only 64K bytes of memory but can address up to one million bytes using segment registers. The Z8000 is also limited to 64K bytes of directly addressable memory; however, the Z8001 version can address as many as 48M bytes of memory using internal segment registers and external segmentation in a memory management device.

Supervisor or
System Modes
and
User or Normal
Modes

5. The MC68000 can be operated in either a "Supervisor" or a "User" mode. Certain privileged instructions can be executed in Supervisor mode only. Supervisor and User modes also have separate stack pointers. Thus, in program-intensive applications, systems software (executed in Supervisor mode) can be separated from applications programs (executed in User mode). The Z8000 series microprocessors provide similar capabilities. The Supervisor mode of the MC68000 is equivalent to the System mode of the Z8000, while the User mode of the MC68000 is equivalent to the Normal mode of the Z8000. The 8086 offers no similar operating modes.

6. The MC68000 has seventeen 32-bit registers. Eight of the registers are designated as Data registers and can be accessed as either 8, 16, or 32-bit registers. The remaining nine registers are designated as Address registers, with two of these being reserved for use as the stack pointers (Supervisor and User). The Address registers can be accessed as 16 or 32-bit registers. All of the registers can also function as Index registers. In contrast, all of the Z8000 registers are 16-bit registers, although they can be paired to operate as 32-bit registers. The 8086 has only four 16-bit registers plus three separate 16-bit Index registers.

7. The MC68000 provides separate pins for every data line and address output line. This is possible since the MC68000 is contained in a 64-pin package and as a result there is no shortage of pin connections. The Z8000 microprocessors and the 8086 are housed in smaller packages and therefore their data and address lines must share some pins. Thus the Z8000 and 8086 devices multiplex some of the data and address signals on the same pins, and you must provide external logic to demultiplex these signals.

The primary source for the MC68000 is:

MOTOROLA SEMICONDUCTOR, INC.
3501 Ed Bluestein Blvd.
Austin, Texas 78721

The MC68000 is manufactured using N-channel HMOS process technology. The device is contained in a dual inline 64-pin package. A single +5 V power supply is required and all signals are TTL-level compatible.

The MC68000 requires an external clock which can be run at a maximum frequency of 8 MHz. The minimum instruction execution time is four clock periods. The maximum number of clock periods for instruction execution is 158 for signed division and multiplication.

SIGNAL CONVENTIONS USED IN THIS BOOK

Signals may be active high, active low or active in two states. An active high signal is one which in the high state causes events to occur, while in the low state has no significance. A signal that is active low causes events to occur when in the low state, but has no significance in the high state. A signal that has two active states will cause two different types of events to occur, depending upon whether the signal is high or low; this signal has no inactive state. Within this book a signal that is active low has a bar placed over the signal name. For example, $\overline{WR}$ identifies a "write strobe" signal which is pulsed low when data is ready for external logic to receive. A signal that is active high or has two active states has no bar over the signal name.

TIMING DIAGRAM CONVENTIONS

Timing diagrams play an important part in the description of any microprocessor or support device. Timing diagrams are therefore used extensively in this book. All timing diagrams observe the following conventions:

1. A low signal level is equivalent to no voltage. A high signal level is equivalent to voltage present:

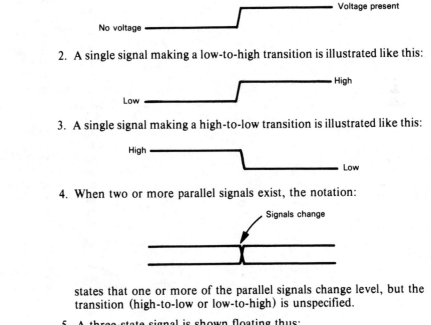

2. A single signal making a low-to-high transition is illustrated like this:

3. A single signal making a high-to-low transition is illustrated like this:

4. When two or more parallel signals exist, the notation:

states that one or more of the parallel signals change level, but the transition (high-to-low or low-to-high) is unspecified.

5. A three-state signal is shown floating thus:

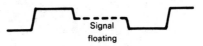

6. A three-state bus containing two or more signals is shown floating thus:

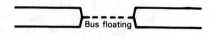

7. When one signal condition triggers other signal changes, an arrow indicates the relationship as follows:

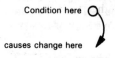

Thus a signal making a low-to-high transition would be illustrated triggering another signal making a high-to-low-transition as follows:

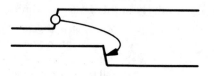

A signal making a high-to-low transition triggering a bus change of state would be illustrated as follows:

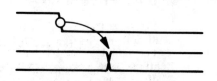

8. When two or more conditions must exist in order to trigger another logic event, the following illustration is used:

Thus a low-to-high transition of one signal occurring while another signal is low would be illustrated triggering a third event as follows:

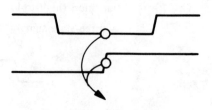

9. When a single triggering condition causes two or more events to occur, the following illustration is used:

Thus a low-to-high transition of one signal triggering changes in two other signal levels would be illustrated as follows:

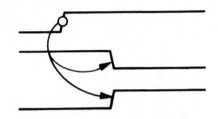

10. All signal level changes are shown as square waves. Thus rise and fall times are ignored. These times are given in the data sheets which appear at the end of this book.

How this Book has been Printed

Notice that text in this book has been printed in boldface type and lightface type. **This has been done to help you skip those parts of the book that cover subject matter with which you are familiar. You can be sure that lightface type only expands on information presented in the previous boldface type.** Therefore, only read boldface type until you reach a subject about which you want to know more, at which point start reading the lightface type.

2

A Functional Overview

PROGRAMMABLE REGISTERS

Figure 2-1 illustrates the registers provided by the MC68000. There are seventeen 32-bit Data and Address registers, a 32-bit Program Counter (of which only 24 bits are used) and a 16-bit Status register. The most significant difference between the registers provided by the MC68000 and those of other 16-bit microprocessors is that the Data and Address registers are all 32 bits wide. By comparison, the 8086 and Z8000 microprocessors use 16-bit wide registers.

Data Registers

The Data registers can be used to handle 8-bit bytes, 16-bit words, or 32-bit long words. The following illustration shows how the various sized operands are positioned within the Data registers.

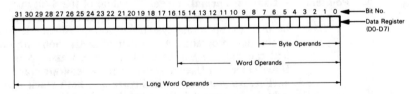

8-bit byte operands occupy bits 0 through 7 of a Data register, while a word operand occupies bits 0 through 15 of a Data register. A long word operand uses all 32 bits of a Data register. When a Data register is used as a source or destination operand, only the appropriate low-order portion of the register will be altered by the specified operation; the more significant bits will be unaffected. For example, if you have specified an arithmetic shift left (ASL)

instruction with an operand size of eight bits, then only the least significant eight bits (bits 0-7) of the Data register will be shifted: bits 8 through 31 will be unchanged by the instruction execution:

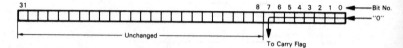

In addition to being used as the source or destination for instructions the Data registers can also be used as index registers or data counters.

Address Registers

There are seven general purpose Address registers (A0-A6). These registers can handle either 16-bit word or 32-bit long word operands. When you use one of these address registers to provide a source operand, either the low-order 16 bits will be used (if a word operand has been specified) or the entire 32 bits will be used (if a long word operand has been specified). If the Address register is used as the source for a word operand, then the more significant 16 bits (bits 16-31) will not be affected. If an Address register is used as the destination operand, however, the contents of the entire register will be affected, regardless of whether a word or long word operand is specified. If you specify a word destination operand for an Address register, that word will be automatically sign-extended to 32 bits before it is loaded into the Address register.

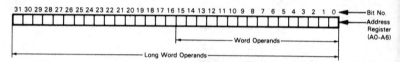

As we have already pointed out, all of the MC68000 Data and Address registers are 32 bits wide, versus the 16-bit wide registers of the Z8000 and 8086. Another significant difference between the MC68000 registers and those of the 8086 is the general purpose nature of the MC68000 registers. This is similar to the approach taken in the Z8000 and provides the programmer with increased flexibility. Although there are minor differences between the way the Data and Address (A0-A6) registers handle various data widths, each register type may be used in similar ways. The only dedicated registers are the Stack Pointer registers (A7, Supervisor and User), the Program Counter and the Status register. Let us now examine these dedicated registers.

Stack Pointers

The MC68000 can be operated in a Supervisor (or system) mode, or in a User (or normal) mode. The state of the S-bit in the Status register determines the mode of operation for the MC68000. Supervisor mode will normally be used by operating system software; User mode will typically be used by application programs. A number of instructions are designated as privileged and can only be executed when the processor is in Supervisor mode. **The Supervisor and User modes also have separate stack pointers, as mentioned earlier. As you can see in Figure 2-1, both stack pointers are addressed as Address register A7.** When the MC68000 is operating in the Supervisor state, the User Stack Pointer cannot be referenced. Conversely, when the MC68000 is in the User state, the Supervisor Stack Pointer cannot be referenced.

Both the User and Supervisor Stack Pointers operate in the same way: the system stacks are filled from high memory to low memory. On subroutine calls the Program Counter contents are pushed onto the appropriate system stack (Supervisor or User). The Program Counter contents will be

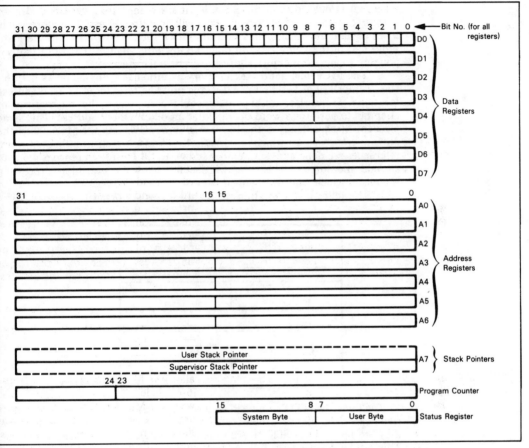

Figure 2-1. Programmable Registers

pulled from the Stack and restored to the Program Counter on return from subroutines. **Since the Program Counter is a 32-bit register, four bytes (two words) of memory will be required to save the contents of the Program Counter on the Stack. The organization of the Program Counter contents on the System Stack after a subroutine call is illustrated as follows:**

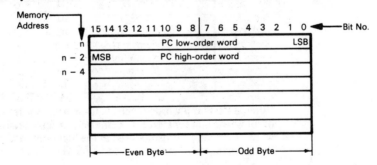

Data that is pushed onto the Stack is always written to a word boundary in memory; that is, to a memory location with an even address. Therefore, when bytes of data must be pushed onto the Stack they are written into the high-order half of the memory word, and the low-order half of that word (corresponding to an odd memory address) will be unchanged.

The MC68000 addresses memory as either 8-bit bytes or as a 16-bit word comprised of two bytes. All words must be referenced at even address locations. Otherwise, misalignment could occur when the microprocessor attempts to perform a word operation at an odd memory address. This same problem exists with any of the 16-bit microprocessors, but the MC68000 is the only microprocessor which automatically checks to ensure that all word references are done at even memory addresses. If a word reference is made to an odd memory address, the MC68000 begins an exception processing sequence, which will be described later.

The following illustration shows how bytes are organized in memory:

```
15 14 13 12 11 10 9  8  7  6  5  4  3  2  1  0  ◄──── Bit No.
┌─────────────────────────┬─────────────────────────┐
│      Byte FFFFFE         │      Byte FFFFFF         │  High Memory
├─────────────────────────┼─────────────────────────┤
│      Byte FFFFFC         │      Byte FFFFFD         │
├─────────────────────────┼─────────────────────────┤
│      Byte FFFFFA         │      Byte FFFFFB         │
├─────────────────────────┼─────────────────────────┤
│      Byte FFFFF8         │      Byte FFFFF9         │
├─────────────────────────┼─────────────────────────┤
│      Byte FFFFF6         │      Byte FFFFF7         │
├─────────────────────────┼─────────────────────────┤
│      Byte FFFFF4         │      Byte FFFFF5         │
└─────────────────────────┴─────────────────────────┘

┌─────────────────────────┬─────────────────────────┐
│      Byte 000006         │      Byte 000007         │
├─────────────────────────┼─────────────────────────┤
│      Byte 000004         │      Byte 000005         │
├─────────────────────────┼─────────────────────────┤
│      Byte 000002         │      Byte 000003         │
├─────────────────────────┼─────────────────────────┤
│      Byte 000000         │      Byte 000001         │  Low Memory
└─────────────────────────┴─────────────────────────┘
```

You will note that the first byte in memory (address 000000) occupies the most significant byte half of a memory word. When words are stored in memory, they are only addressable at even memory addresses, as we have discussed. This can be illustrated as follows:

```
15 14 13 12 11 10 9  8  7  6  5  4  3  2  1  0  ◄──── Bit No.
┌───────────────────────────────────────────────────┐
│                   Word FFFFFE                      │  High Memory
├───────────────────────────────────────────────────┤
│                   Word FFFFFC                      │
├───────────────────────────────────────────────────┤
│                   Word FFFFFA                      │
├───────────────────────────────────────────────────┤
│                   Word FFFFF8                      │
├───────────────────────────────────────────────────┤
│                   Word FFFFF6                      │
├───────────────────────────────────────────────────┤
│                   Word FFFFF4                      │
└───────────────────────────────────────────────────┘

┌───────────────────────────────────────────────────┐
│                   Word 000006                      │
├───────────────────────────────────────────────────┤
│                   Word 000004                      │
├───────────────────────────────────────────────────┤
│                   Word 000002                      │
├───────────────────────────────────────────────────┤
│                   Word 000000                      │  Low Memory
└───────────────────────────────────────────────────┘
```

When 32-bit long words (such as 32-bit addresses) are stored in memory, they occupy two adjacent 16-bit memory locations or four bytes. The high-order word of the long words is stored at the higher memory location, as illustrated in the following diagram.

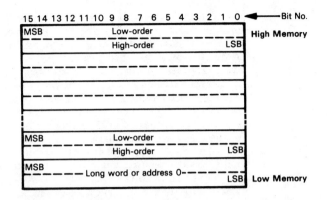

The MC68000 provides a 16-bit Status register which is divided into two 8-bit bytes: the System byte and the User byte. Figure 2-2 shows the bit assignments for the Status register. The Carry, Overflow, Zero, and Negative bits are the standard ones provided by most microprocessors.

The Carry (C) bit is set if there is a carry out of the most significant bit following an addition operation, or if a borrow is required from the most significant bit during a subtraction. This status bit is also modified by certain shift and rotate instructions.

The Overflow (V) bit is the exclusive-OR of the carries out of the most significant and next higher-order bits of the operand following arithmetic operations. The setting of the Overflow bit signifies a magnitude overflow since the result cannot be represented in the specified operand size.

The Zero (Z) bit is set whenever the result of an operation is zero; it is reset otherwise.

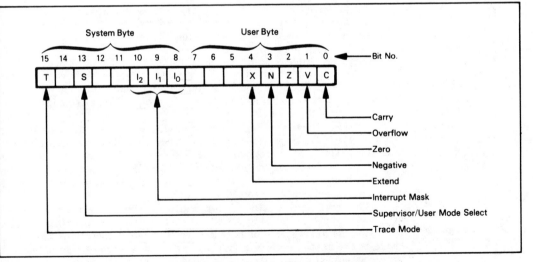

Figure 2-2. Status Register Bit Assignments

The **Negative (N) bit** is the equivalent of the Sign status bit provided in most microprocessors. The Negative bit **is equal to the value of the most significant result bit following arithmetic operations.** If a signed binary arithmetic operation is being performed, a Negative status of 0 specifies a positive or zero result, whereas a Negative status of 1 specifies a negative result.

The **Extend (X) bit is used in multiprecision arithmetic operations. When it is affected by an instruction, it is set to the same state as the Carry bit.**

The **three most significant bits (bits 5, 6, and 7) of the User byte of the Status register are not currently assigned and will always be zero.**

The **System byte of the Status register contains status information that is system-related. The User byte, on the other hand, contains the Condition Code status bits (X, N, Z, V, and C) that are instruction or program related. Bits in the System byte of the Status register can only be altered when the MC68000 is in the Supervisor mode.**

Interrupt Mask The **three least significant bits (bits 8, 9, and 10) of the Status register's System byte form the interrupt mask.** The MC68000 provides seven levels of interrupts. The level of any given interrupt is decoded from the signal's three interrupt pins, which we will describe later. **The interrupt priorities are numbered from 1 to 7, with level 7 having the highest priority, as shown in the following illustration:**

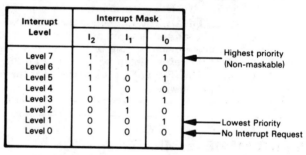

Interrupt Level	Interrupt Mask		
	I_2	I_1	I_0
Level 7	1	1	1
Level 6	1	1	0
Level 5	1	0	1
Level 4	1	0	0
Level 3	0	1	1
Level 2	0	1	0
Level 1	0	0	1
Level 0	0	0	0

Level 7 → Highest priority (Non-maskable)
Level 1 → Lowest Priority
Level 0 → No Interrupt Request

The level 7 interrupt is nonmaskable and thus cannot be disabled. Level 0 represents a ''no interrupt request'' condition. Levels 1 through 6 are the mask-enabled levels. For example, if you set the mask to 100 then only levels 5, 6, and 7 will be enabled; interrupt levels 1 through 4 are disabled and interrupt requests of those levels will be ignored.

S-bit in Status Register Bit 13 of the Status register is the S-bit, which specifies whether the MC68000 is in the Supervisor or User mode of operation. When this bit is 1, the MC68000 is in the Supervisor mode, and when it is 0 the microprocessor is in the User mode. Recall that the Supervisor and User modes have their own separate stack pointers; also, certain privileged instructions can only be executed in the Supervisor mode.

Trace Mode (T) Bit in Status Register The most significant bit of the Status register is the Trace mode (T) flag. If this bit is 0 then the MC68000 operates normally. **If this bit is 1, however, the microprocessor is in the Trace mode of operation. The Trace mode is the approximate software equivalent of a hardware implemented single-step mode.** After each instruction is executed in the Trace mode, a trap is forced so that a debugging program can monitor the results of that instruction's execution.

Table 2-1. Addressing Mode Summary

Mode	Address Formation
Register Direct Addressing Data Register Direct Address Register Direct	EA = DREGn EA = AREGn
Register Indirect Addressing Register Indirect Postincrement Register Indirect Predecrement Register Indirect Register Indirect with Offset Indexed Register Indirect with Offset	EA = (AREGn) EA = (AREGn); Increment (AREGn) Decrement (AREGn); EA = (AREGn) EA = (AREGn) + data16 EA = (AREGn) + (XREGn) + data8
Implied Register Addressing	EA = SR, SP, PC
Absolute Addressing Absolute Short Absolute Long	EA = (Next word) EA = (Next 2 words)
Program Counter Relative Addressing Relative with Offset Relative with Index and Offset	EA = (PC) + data16 EA = (PC) + (XREG) + data8
Immediate Data Addressing Immediate Quick Immediate	Data = Next word or words Data inherent in instruction word

EA = Effective Address DREGn = Any Data Register AREGn = Any Address Register XREGn = Any Data or Address Register used as an Index Register ( ) = Contents of	data8 = 8-bit offset (displacement) data16 = 16-bit offset (displacement) SR = Status Register SP = Stack Pointer (User or Supervisor) PC = Program Counter

ADDRESSING MODE SUMMARY

The MC68000 provides six basic types of addressing modes. Variations within these types allow a total of fourteen different modes, as summarized in Table 2-1. At this point, we will look only briefly at the addressing modes and how they utilize the registers of the MC68000. We will discuss each of the addressing modes in detail in Chapter 5.

Most of the addressing modes use the 32-bit Address registers either directly or indirectly to generate the effective address. The Data registers can be used as sources for addresses in the direct addressing mode, and they can also be used as index registers in some of the indirect addressing modes. The indirect addressing modes include post-incrementing or pre-decrementing of an Address register; this capability makes it easy to implement stacks and queues in memory.

A number of MC68000 instructions use the implied addressing mode; that is, they make implicit reference to either the Program Counter (PC), Stack Pointer (SP) or Status Register (SR). For example, Branch, Jump, and Return instructions will all reference the Program Counter and Stack Pointer during their execution.

Absolute addressing modes do not utilize the Data or Address registers, but instead form the effective address using data that follows the instruction word in the program. Program Counter relative addressing can use either a displacement or a displacement plus the contents of an Index register to form the effective address. The Index register can be any of the Data or Address registers.

Most instructions can utilize any of the addressing modes, and address formation is always the same, regardless of the instruction operation itself. These factors do much to enhance the flexibility and power of the instruction set without making the instruction set difficult to understand.

PINS AND SIGNALS

Figure 2-3 illustrates the signals and pin assignments for the MC68000. At this point, we will briefly discuss each of these signals to provide an overview of how the MC68000 operates. We will defer a detailed discussion of signal and timing interactions until later in this chapter.

Data Bus

D0-D15 is the bidirectional 16-bit Data Bus. A1-A23 is the output 24-bit Address Bus. Because the MC68000 is contained in a 64-pin package, the data and address lines need not be multiplexed onto the same pins, as is the case with the 8086 and Z8000 microprocessors. Note that **A0, the least significant bit of the Address Bus, is not output;** this bit is used internal to the MC68000, in conjunction with the data size specification of each instruction, to generate the $\overline{\text{UDS}}$ and $\overline{\text{LDS}}$ signals.

Address Bus

Data Strobes

The $\overline{\text{UDS}}$ (Upper Data Strobe) and $\overline{\text{LDS}}$ (Lower Data Strobe) signals **determine whether data is being transferred on either the upper (most significant) byte, the lower (least significant) byte, or both bytes of the 16-bit Data Bus. Table 2-2 defines the significance of the $\overline{\text{UDS}}$, $\overline{\text{LDS}}$, and Read/Write (R/$\overline{\text{W}}$) signals in relation to the Data Bus.** When $\overline{\text{UDS}}$ is low, data from memory with an even address is accessed and the byte of data is transferred on D8-D15. When $\overline{\text{LDS}}$ is low, a byte of data located at an odd address is accessed and the transfer occurs on D0-D7. When the MC68000 is transferring a word of data (for example, when fetching an instruction) then both $\overline{\text{UDS}}$ and $\overline{\text{LDS}}$ will be low and all 16 of the data lines (D0-D15) will be used for the transfer.

Table 2-2. Data Bus Control Signal Summary

$\overline{\text{UDS}}$	$\overline{\text{LDS}}$	R/$\overline{\text{W}}$	D8-D15	D0-D7	Operation
High	High				
Low	Low	High	Data bits 8-15	Data bits 0-7	Word Read
High	Low	High		Data bits 0-7	Byte Read
Low	High	High	Data bits 8-15		Byte Read
Low	Low	Low	Data bits 8-15	Data bits 0-7	Word Write
High	Low	Low	Data bits 0-7	Data bits 0-7	Byte Write
Low	High	Low	Data bits 8-15	Data bits 8-15	Byte Write

▨ No valid data output or input

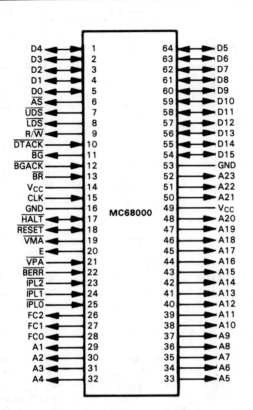

Pin Name	Description	Type
D0-D15	Data Bus	Bidirectional, Tristate
A1-A23	Address Bus	Output, Tristate
$\overline{AS}$	Address Strobe	Output, Tristate
R/$\overline{W}$	Read/Write Control	Output, Tristate
$\overline{UDS}$, $\overline{LDS}$	Upper, Lower Data Strobes	Output, Tristate
$\overline{DTACK}$	Data Transfer Acknowledge	Input
FC0, FC1, FC2	Function Code (status) Outputs	Output, Tristate
$\overline{IPL0}$, $\overline{IPL1}$, $\overline{IPL2}$	Interrupt Requests	Input
$\overline{BERR}$	Bus Error	Input
$\overline{HALT}$	Halt Processor Operation	Input/Output
$\overline{RESET}$	Reset Processor or Reset External Devices	Input/Output
CLK	System Clock	Input
$\overline{BR}$	Bus Request	Input
$\overline{BG}$	Bus Grant	Output
$\overline{BGACK}$	Bus Grant Acknowledge	Input
E	Enable (Clock) Output	Output
$\overline{VMA}$	Valid Memory Address	Output, Tristate
$\overline{VPA}$	Valid Peripheral Address	Input
V_{CC}, GND	Power (+5 V) and Ground	

Figure 2-3. Pins and Signal Assignments

Table 2-3. Function Code Summary

FC2	FC1	FC0	Machine Cycle Type
0	0	0	
0	0	1	User data memory access
0	1	0	User program memory access
0	1	1	
1	0	0	
1	0	1	Supervisor data memory access
1	1	0	Supervisor program memory access
1	1	1	Interrupt acknowledge

Reserved, currently undefined

Memory Interface

The memory interface implied by the $\overline{\text{UDS}}$ and $\overline{\text{LDS}}$ signals is illustrated in **Figure 2-4.** Byte-oriented memory with even addresses will be selected by $\overline{\text{UDS}}$, and that memory's data lines are connected to D8-D15. $\overline{\text{LDS}}$ references byte memory with odd addresses, and its data will be applied to D0-D7 of the Data Bus. The $\overline{\text{AS}}$ line, shown in Figure 2-4, is the Address Strobe which is pulsed low to indicate that a valid data address is being output on the Address Bus (A1-A23).

Data Transfer Acknowledge Signal

$\overline{\text{DTACK}}$ is the Data Transfer Acknowledge input signal. This signal must be asserted by external logic during every read or write cycle. When the MC68000 is performing a read or write cycle, it will automatically insert wait states in the cycle until the $\overline{\text{DTACK}}$ signal is received. This approach is thus the inverse of the logic used by most other microprocessors: for example, both the Z8000 and 8086 have a "wait" input which external logic can use to extend a read or write cycle — if the wait input is not asserted, the read/write cycle will finish normally. The MC68000 approach provides for completely asynchronous bus operations that can interface to any type of device regardless of that device's speed. This approach specifies, however, that **all devices in the system must include sufficient logic to generate the $\overline{\text{DTACK}}$ signal.**

Function Code Outputs

FC0, FC1, and FC2 are the Function Code or processor cycle status outputs. These outputs identify the type of bus activity currently being performed by the MC68000, as summarized in Table 2-3. The Function Code outputs are valid whenever $\overline{\text{AS}}$ is true. **Five different types of cycles are currently defined: access to either supervisor data memory, supervisor program memory, user data memory, or user program memory, and interrupt acknowledge cycles.** Whenever the MC68000 is involved in fetching instructions, it is considered as accessing program memory. All other memory accesses are identified as data memory accesses. The Function Code outputs could be used to separate memory into the four different categories — user versus supervisor and program versus data. Thus, by using the FC outputs an MC68000 system could directly address up to 64 megabytes of memory, with 16 megabytes devoted to each of the four defined memory categories.

Interrupt Requests

$\overline{\text{IPL0}}$, $\overline{\text{IPL1}}$, and $\overline{\text{IPL2}}$ are the interrupt request inputs. These three inputs are decoded internally by the MC68000 to determine the priority level of the interrupt request. You will recall from our earlier discussion of the

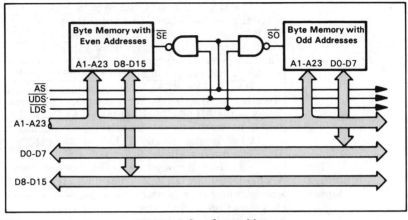

Figure 2-4. Interface to Memory

Status register that there is a 3-bit interrupt mask which determines what level of interrupt request will be permitted. When all three interrupt inputs are low, a non-maskable interrupt (level 7, which is the highest priority) is present. This level is always recognized by the MC68000. When all three of the interrupt inputs are high, it indicates that no interrupt is being requested.

Bus Error Input

$\overline{BERR}$ **is the Bus Error input. When this signal is low the MC68000 performs a sequence (exception processing sequence) similar to that which it executes in response to an interrupt request. The purpose of the $\overline{BERR}$ signal is to inform the MC68000 when an external device has not responded (using the $\overline{DTACK}$ input) within an expected amount of time during a read or write operation.** Since the data transfer handshaking approach used by the MC68000 requires all external devices to actively respond to every data transfer, the system should include a mechanism to ensure that the processor is not hung up indefinitely by a device that fails to respond. Thus external logic should be provided to monitor bus activity, utilizing the $\overline{BERR}$ signal to inform the MC68000 of a "failure to respond" condition. This logic would separate the preceding cause of a bus error from other causes, such as might be generated with a Memory Management Unit (MMU). The MMU would generate $\overline{BERR}$ if an attempt was made to access protected memory.

As we have already mentioned, the reaction of the MC68000 to the Bus Error input is similar to the interrupt request response. We will describe this response, termed "exception processing," in detail later in this chapter. Essentially, exception processing causes processor status information to be saved, and then allows the processor to execute a program to analyze the cause of the error. The MC68000 also provides a hardware-oriented response to a bus error: **if the $\overline{HALT}$ signal is asserted in conjunction with the $\overline{BERR}$ signal, the MC68000 will automatically retry the bus cycle that produced the error.**

The Halt Signal

The $\overline{HALT}$ signal performs several functions. As we mentioned in the preceding paragraph, **it can be used in conjunction with the $\overline{BERR}$ signal to initiate rerunning of bus cycles** that produced bus errors. When used alone, it places the MC68000 in a Halt state where the processor is essentially inactive until the $\overline{HALT}$ signal is negated. This is the familiar Halt function provided by most microprocessors.

The $\overline{\text{HALT}}$ signal is also used in conjunction with the $\overline{\text{RESET}}$ signal to intialize the MC68000. One unusual aspect of the $\overline{\text{RESET}}$ signal is the fact that it is also an ouput signal; **the MC68000 provides a RESET instruction which, when executed, causes a low-going pulse to be output on the $\overline{\text{RESET}}$ pin.** Thus, you can execute a RESET instruction and use it to initialize other devices in the system without resetting the processor.

$\overline{\text{HALT}}$, like $\overline{\text{RESET}}$, **is an output signal. If the processor ceases executing instructions — for example, if a double bus fault condition occurs — the MC68000 will output $\overline{\text{HALT}}$ low.** External logic can then be used to detect this potentially catastrophic condition.

CLK is the single TTL-level compatible clock from which all MC68000 internal timing is derived.

$\overline{\text{BR}}$ **(Bus Request),** $\overline{\text{BG}}$ **(Bus Grant), and** $\overline{\text{BGACK}}$ **(Bus Grant Acknowledge) are all bus arbitration signals.** These signals are used in systems where other devices, such as DMA controllers on other processors, require control of the System Busses. **External devices request access to the System Bus by asserting the** $\overline{\text{BR}}$ **input. The MC68000 will then always relin-**quish the bus after it has completed the current bus cycle. **It will also output Bus Grant** ($\overline{\text{BG}}$) **low to let the requesting device know that the bus will become available at the end of the current cycle.** However, as we will see when we discuss the bus arbitration timing in detail, external devices or logic must monitor more than just the Bus Grant signal to determine when the bus will actually be available. **The Bus Grant Acknowledge** ($\overline{\text{BGACK}}$) **signal must be input to the MC68000 by the device requesting the bus once that device takes control of the bus.** $\overline{\text{BGACK}}$ must be held low until the device has completed its bus access operations. Thus $\overline{\text{BGACK}}$ is essentially a "bus busy" signal that lets the MC68000 (and other devices in the system) know that the bus is unavailable.

The next three signals — E, $\overline{\text{VPA}}$**, and** $\overline{\text{VMA}}$ **— are provided so that the MC68000 can be easily interfaced to the standard and widely available 6800 family devices.** 6800-based systems use a synchronous method of effecting transfers of data throughout the system. To accomplish this a system clock Enable (E) signal must be distributed to all 6800 devices in the system so that all relevant data transfers may be synchronized to this clock signal. **Thus the Enable (E) signal provided by the MC68000 is the equivalent of the 6800 E signal.** The frequency of E is equal to one-tenth that of the CLK input to the MC68000: the period for E is equal to 10 CLK periods — E is low for six CLK cycles and is high for four CLK cycles.

The Valid Peripheral Address ($\overline{\text{VPA}}$) **signal is used by 6800-type devices in the system to inform the MC68000 that a 6800-type data transfer is required.** You must provide address decoding logic in the system that determines when a 6800-type device is being accessed and that generates the $\overline{\text{VPA}}$ signal. **When the MC68000 receives the** $\overline{\text{VPA}}$ **signal, it alters the data transfer timing so that it is synchronous with the Enable (E) signal. The MC68000 will then output the Valid Memory Address** ($\overline{\text{VMA}}$) **signal at the appropriate time.** $\overline{\text{VMA}}$ is another 6800-type signal and will only be output if the $\overline{\text{VPA}}$ input signal has been asserted at the beginning of a data transfer operation. We will defer a detailed discussion of these three signals until later when we describe interfacing between the MC68000 and the 6800-family devices.

3

Timing and Bus Operation

The basic timing for the MC68000 is quite straightforward: instruction execution consists of a combination of internal cycles and bus access cycles. The total number of clock cycles required for each instruction is defined in the instruction set summary tables later in this chapter. The number of clock cycles required to perform operations internal to the MC68000 are of little interest to other devices in the system since these operations are transparent to external logic. It is only when the MC68000 requires access to the system bus for such operations as instruction fetching, operand fetching, and operand storing that external devices become involved with MC68000 timing.

The MC68000 uses memory mapped I/O. Therefore, bus accesses for data transfers between the MC68000 and memory are the same as for those between the MC68000 and I/O devices. Data transfers are defined as either read or write operations, with the transfer of data into the MC68000 defined as a "read" and the transfer of data from the MC68000 to external logic defined as a "write."

Read Timing

Figure 3-1 illustrates the timing for a read word operation. For purposes of the following timing discussions, each clock period is sub-divided into two states.

During state 0 (S0) of the read word cycle, the address and data busses are in the high impedance state — the MC68000 is not using the System Bus at this point. Address information for the memory or I/O location is output at the beginning of state 1 (S1) on the Address Bus (A1-A23). Processor cycle status information is also output at this point on the FC0-FC2 pins. The Address Strobe (AS) signal is asserted at the beginning of state 2 and can be used by external logic to latch the information on the Address Bus. Simultaneously, the Upper Data Strobe (UDS) and Lower Data Strobe (LDS) signals are asserted to enable selection of both the most significant byte and least significant byte of

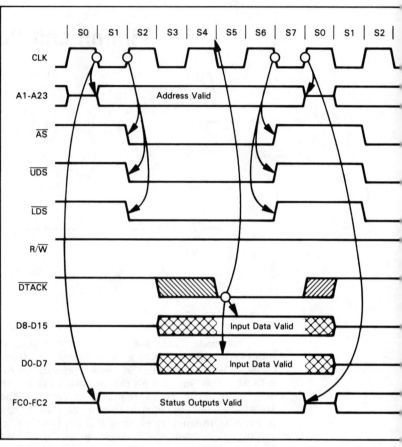

Figure 3-1. Read Word Timing

a 16-bit word. You will note that these signals are not actually data "strobes" since there is no data ready to be input or output at this point; it is more accurate to think of them as memory select signals selecting the upper and/or lower byte of a 16-bit memory word. R/$\overline{W}$ is normally asserted, so this output does not change during a read cycle.

The MC68000 now waits for the addressed memory or I/O device to present its data on the Data Bus. When the data is ready, the external device must assert Data Acknowledge ($\overline{DTACK}$) to the MC68000. The MC68000 expects $\overline{DTACK}$ and the requested data to be present by state 5 (S5). If $\overline{DTACK}$ is not present by S5, Wait states (SW) will be automatically inserted into the read timing cycle as illustrated in Figure 3-2. Once $\overline{DTACK}$ is true, the read cycle continues with S5. At the end of state 6 (S6), the $\overline{AS}$, $\overline{UDS}$, and $\overline{LDS}$ signals are negated. At this point the incoming data on D0-D15 is latched into an internal MC68000 register. External devices can use the negative-to-positive transition of $\overline{AS}$, $\overline{UDS}$, or $\overline{LDS}$ as the indication that they can remove data from the Data Bus. The MC68000 maintains the address information and function code information through the end of state 7 (S7) to allow for signal skew within the system. Note that when the external device senses that the

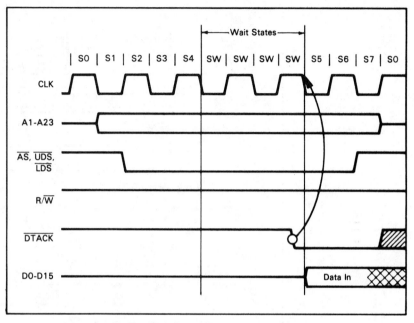

Figure 3-2. Wait States During Read Operations

MC68000 has captured the data from the Data Bus (by sensing the high-going transition of $\overline{AS}$, $\overline{UDS}$, or $\overline{LDS}$) that device must return $\overline{DTACK}$ high immediately so that it does not interfere with the beginning of the next bus cycle.

Wait State
    If you refer to the Wait state insertion that can occur during read operations, as illustrated in Figure 3-2, you will see that the Wait states occur between state 4 and state 5. The MC68000 will maintain valid address output on the Address Bus and will hold $\overline{AS}$, $\overline{UDS}$, and $\overline{LDS}$ low during any Wait states for as long as necessary until $\overline{DTACK}$ is asserted. You should note that there will always be an even number of Wait states inserted; all MC68000 operations are based on a complete CLK cycle and there are two "states" per CLK cycle.

Read Byte Timing
    Timing for a read byte operation is illustrated in Figure 3-3. This figure shows first an even data byte and then an odd data byte being read by the MC68000. As you can see, the only difference between this timing and that illustrated for a read word operation in Figure 3-1 is that only $\overline{UDS}$ or $\overline{LDS}$ is asserted and only eight lines of the Data Bus are utilized when you are reading a byte: $\overline{UDS}$ is asserted and data is on lines D8-D15 when reading a byte located at an even address, and $\overline{LDS}$ is asserted and data is on lines D0-D7 when reading a byte located at an odd address. You should not be misled by Figure 3-3 into thinking that the MC68000 always reads two consecutive bytes — an even byte and an odd byte. We have simply shown these two read operations consecutively to illustrate timing for both. Again, if the MC68000 requires a word of data, it will utilize the entire 16-bit Data Bus and read the full word in one operation.

Write Timing
    Timing for a write word operation is illustrated in Figure 3-4. As was the case with read operations, the address for the memory location or I/O device is output at the beginning of S1 along with the appropriate function code

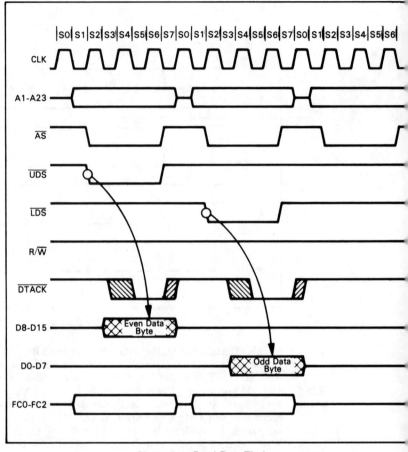

Figure 3-3. Read Byte Timing

indicating the current type of processor bus cycle. If the Data Bus was utilized by the MC68000 in the preceding cycle, the processor returns all of the data outputs to the high impedance state during S1 and then asserts the Address Strobe ($\overline{\text{AS}}$) signal and outputs the Read/Write (R/$\overline{\text{W}}$) signal low. Once again $\overline{\text{AS}}$ can be used to latch the address externally, and the R/$\overline{\text{W}}$ signal indicates to memory or I/O devices that the MC68000 will be placing data onto the Data Bus. No further signal activity occurs until the MC68000 outputs the data on D0-D15 at the beginning of state 3 (S3). The Upper and Lower Data Strobe signals ($\overline{\text{UDS}}$, $\overline{\text{LDS}}$) are asserted at the beginning of state 4 (S4). During write operations, these two signals can be used as "strobe" signals since they indicate that the data on the Data Bus is valid. If the write operation is to proceed unimpeded, external logic must respond to the data strobe signals by asserting the Data Acknowledge ($\overline{\text{DTACK}}$) signal by the beginning of state 7 (S7). If

"Slow Writes" $\overline{\text{DTACK}}$ **is not true by the beginning of S7, Wait states are automatically inserted by the MC68000, as illustrated in Figure 3-5. This "slow write" operation is the same as was illustrated for read operations except that the Wait states are inserted at a different point in the cycle.**

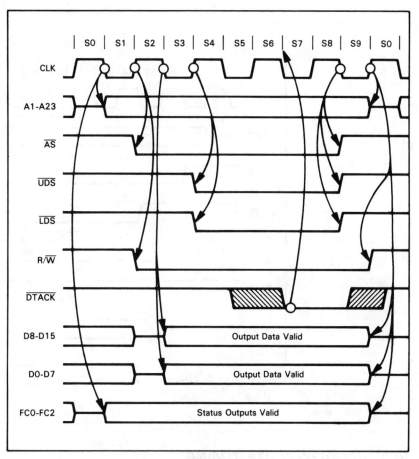

Figure 3-4. Write Word Timing

The MC68000 outputs the data on D0-D15 through the entire write operation. The address strobe ($\overline{AS}$) and data strobes ($\overline{UDS}$, $\overline{LDS}$) are negated at the beginning of state 9 (S9) and the Read/Write (R/$\overline{W}$) signal is returned high at the end of S9. At that point, the Address Bus, Data Bus, and Function Code outputs are all returned to their high impedance state to free the System Bus for other uses. The external memory or I/O device that was accessed by the write operation must release the Data Acknowledge ($\overline{DTACK}$) signal after it has detected the positive-to-negative transition of the address or data strobe signals. This ensures that a subsequent bus cycle will not be impeded.

Write Byte Timing   **Timing for write byte operation is illustrated in Figure 3-6.** As you can see, the only difference between this operation and the write word timing illustrated in Figure 3-4 is the fact that only $\overline{UDS}$ or $\overline{LDS}$ is output while a byte is being written.

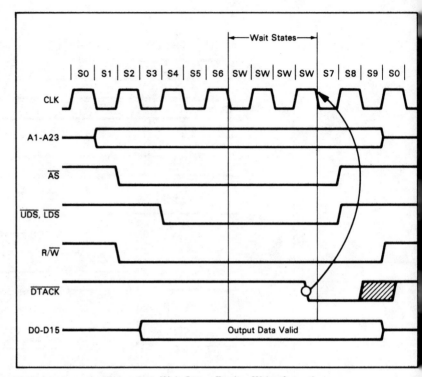

Figure 3-5. Wait States During Write Operations

READ-MODIFY-WRITE TIMING

**Test and
Set (TAS)
Instruction**

The read-modify-write cycle provided by the MC68000 is unusual among microprocessors, although it is frequently provided by minicomputers. The MC68000 uses the read-modify-write cycle only during the execution of the Test and Set (TAS) instruction. This instruction reads a byte of data, sets condition codes according to the contents of that byte, sets bit 7 of the byte, and then writes it back into memory. The TAS instruction is intended to be used as a means of providing "safe" communication between microprocessors in a multi-processor system. Safe communication is ensured with the TAS instruction since the read-modify-write cycle is non-interruptable.

Figure 3-7 illustrates the timing for a read-modify-write cycle. As you can see, it simply consists of the read-byte cycle followed by a standard write-byte cycle. There is one intervening clock period (S8, S9) between the read and write cycles and it is during this interval that the byte of data is modified internally for the subsequent write. Just as was the case with standard read and write, external logic must reply with $\overline{\text{DTACK}}$ at the proper time or else Wait states will automatically be inserted to lengthen the read or write operations.

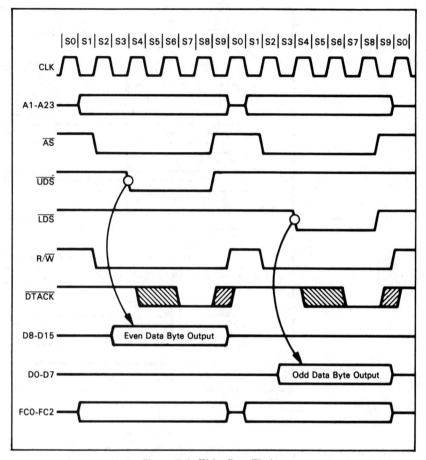

Figure 3-6. Write Byte Timing

Note that in Figure 3-7 we have shown that either $\overline{UDS}$ or $\overline{LDS}$ will be asserted during the read-modify-write operation. This is because the TAS instruction always operates on a byte of data, never on a word of data.

THE RESET OPERATION

The MC68000 has an asynchronous reset input. You reset the microprocessor by holding the $\overline{RESET}$ and $\overline{HALT}$ signals low for at least 100 milliseconds. After the $\overline{RESET}$ and $\overline{HALT}$ signals are returned high, the MC68000 executes the following operations:

1. The MC68000 reads the first four words from memory (bytes 000000 through 000007) and uses the contents of these locations to load the

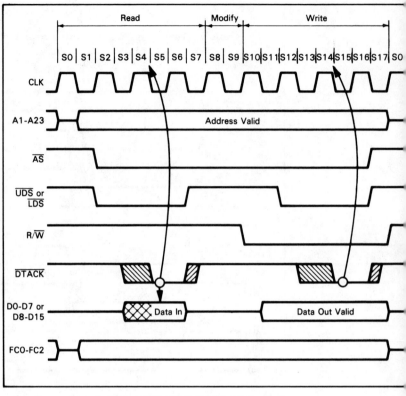

Figure 3-7. Read-Modify-Write Timing

System Stack Pointer (SSP) and Program Counter (PC). The content of these eight bytes from the beginning of memory are used a follows:

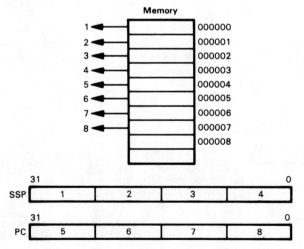

2. The interrupt mask in the Status register is set to all ones so that only level 7 interrupts will be enabled. No other registers are affected by the reset operation: therefore, when a reset is performed after applying power to the MC68000, all registers except SSP, PC, and the Status register will contain indeterminate values.

3. Program execution begins, with the first instruction being fetched from the location indicated by the value loaded into the Program Counter.

The Reset Instruction

The sequence we just described is the typical externally-initiated reset operation similar to that provided by most microprocessors. You will recall, however, that the $\overline{\text{RESET}}$ pin is bidirectional; when the MC68000 executes a Reset instruction, a low-going pulse is sent out on the $\overline{\text{RESET}}$ pin. This software $\overline{\text{RESET}}$ pulse is low for 124 CLK cycles. This instruction has no effect on the internal state of the MC68000; therefore, none of its internal registers is affected. In this case, the $\overline{\text{RESET}}$ signal is being used to reset all other devices within the system under the control of the MC68000.

HE HALT STATE

The MC68000 can be forced into a Halt state, at which time its Address Bus, Data Bus, and Function Code outputs (FC0-FC2) are placed in the high-impedance state. This state is similar to the Hold state of the 8086 and the Stop state of the Z8000. The Halt state can be used to disable the MC68000 and thus free the System Busses for such activities as direct memory access or multi-processor operations. However, since the MC68000 includes an efficient bus arbitration system, it is more likely that the Halt state will be used to implement a hardware single-step mode.

Halt Timing

Figure 3-8 illustrates the timing for the Halt operation. If the MC68000 is in the middle of a bus cycle when the $\overline{\text{HALT}}$ signal is input low, the bus cycle continues to its normal completion. At the end of the cycle the Address Bus, Data Bus, and FC0-FC2 signals are all placed in the high impedance state and the MC68000 halts. While it is in this halted condition, the processor does nothing — it merely waits for the $\overline{\text{HALT}}$ signal to return high. Note that the MC68000 provides no halt acknowledge indication to external logic.

However, while the MC68000 is in the Halt state, its bus arbitration circuitry still operates. Since the MC68000 will not be using the bus while it is halted, any bus request made to the MC68000 will be granted immediately. We will defer a detailed discussion of the bus arbitration circuitry until later.

When the $\overline{\text{HALT}}$ signal is returned high, the MC68000 exits the Halt state within two clock cycles and can then begin another bus cycle.

Single-Stepping with $\overline{\text{HALT}}$

The execution of most MC68000 instructions requires multiple bus cycles to fetch the instruction and operands and, possibly, to store results of the instruction. **Since the MC68000 will respond to the $\overline{\text{HALT}}$ input upon completion of any bus cycle, the halt sequence can occur between two instructions or in the middle of a single instruction. Therefore, if you are using the $\overline{\text{HALT}}$ input to implement a single-step mode of operation, you will be single-stepping by bus cycles rather than single-stepping by instructions.** If you want to single-step by instructions, you must use the Trace function of the MC68000. This function is implemented by setting the T-bit in the Supervisor byte of the Status register. We will describe the Trace operation in detail later.

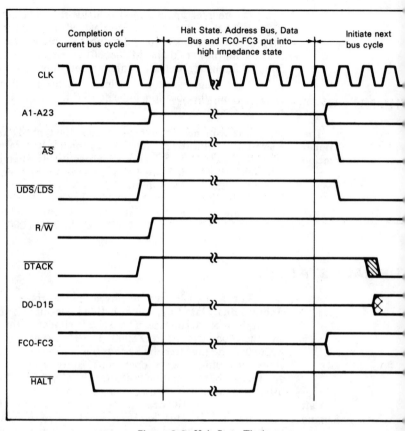

Figure 3-8. Halt State Timing

HALT
Output
Signal

The $\overline{\text{HALT}}$ signal is bidirectional and will be asserted by the MC68000 if it initiates a Halt state rather than having external logic cause the Halt. The MC68000 will automatically enter the Halt state if there is a double-bus fault (we will discuss bus errors and double-bus faults in detail later). If the MC68000 has automatically entered the Halt state, the processor will output $\overline{\text{HALT}}$ low and remain in this halted condition until an externally initiated reset operation is performed using $\overline{\text{RESET}}$. Thus, when $\overline{\text{HALT}}$ is output low by the MC68000, it indicates a catastrophic failure.

THE STOP STATE

The
STOP
Instruction

Following execution of the STOP instruction, the MC68000 microprocessor will enter a Stop state. The STOP instruction is permitted only when the MC68000 is operating in the Supervisor mode as indicated by the S-bit in the Status register. The Stop state is similar to the Halt state which we just discussed, since the microprocessor essentially does nothing while in this state. When the STOP instruction is executed, the Status register is loaded with a new value contained in the instruction. Next, the Program Counter is advanced to point to the next instruction and the MC68000 stops

No special signal or status is output by the MC68000 to identify that it is in the Stop state. The Stop state is ended by one of the exception conditions such as an interrupt request or a RESET. When an exception condition is detected by the MC68000, it leaves the Stop state and will process the exception condition.

THE BUS CYCLE RERUN TIMING

As we mentioned earlier, the MC68000 can respond in two ways to a System Bus error, indicated by the assertion of BERR. It can perform exception processing (which we will describe later), or it can attempt to rerun the bus cycle which caused the bus error indication. If BERR is asserted by itself, then the exception processing (or software) method of handling the bus error is taken. However, if the BERR signal is accompanied by the HALT signal

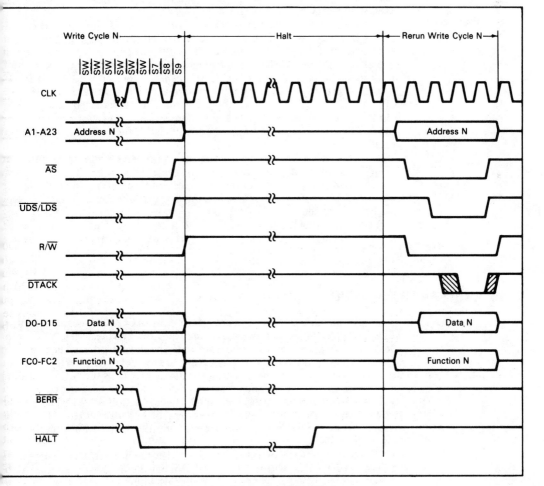

Figure 3-9. Rerun Bus Cycle Timing

then the MC68000 recognizes this as a request to rerun the bus cycle.

Figure 3-9 illustrates the timing for the bus cycle rerun operation. this figure, we have shown a write cycle in progress, with the MC68000 waitin for the external device to respond with $\overline{\text{DTACK}}$ so that the cycle can be cor .pleted. Instead of the expected acknowledge signal, external logic forces bo the $\overline{\text{BERR}}$ and $\overline{\text{HALT}}$ signals low to indicate that the cycle was not successful completed and that the MC68000 should rerun the cycle.

The MC68000 proceeds to complete the cycle that was in progress ar then enters the $\overline{\text{HALT}}$ state. The Address Bus, Data Bus, and Function Co outputs are all placed in the high impedance state and the microprocess remains halted until both $\overline{\text{BERR}}$ and $\overline{\text{HALT}}$ are negated. Note that BER should be negated before $\overline{\text{HALT}}$ is negated to prevent the MC68000 fro interpreting the isolated $\overline{\text{BERR}}$ signal as another bus error — one that expected to be handled in software. After $\overline{\text{HALT}}$ returns high, the MC680 will proceed to repeat the cycle that was in progress when the rerun request w received; i.e., the same address, data, and function code information that w used in the previous bus cycle will be repeated.

Successful
Rerun
Operation

Figure 3-9 shows the successful completion of the rerun cycle wi DTACK being received in the expected interval. Of course, this will n always be the case — the attempt to rerun the bus cycle might also result in bus error. **External logic can continue to request that the cycle be rerun a unlimited number of times, using the combination of $\overline{\text{BERR}}$ and HAL** You should note, however, that if you are using the software exception pr cessing method of handling the bus error ($\overline{\text{BERR}}$ asserted alone witho $\overline{\text{HALT}}$), then two successive bus errors are treated as a catastrophic error ar the MC68000 will automatically enter the Halt state and remain there un reset.

If the MC68000 is performing a read-modify-write cycle and a b error is encountered, it will not rerun the cycle. This is done because the rea modify-write is only used during the Test and Set ($\overline{\text{TAS}}$) instruction. Tr nature of this instruction demands complete execution cycle integrity, whic might be violated if any of the bus cycles were repeated. If external log requests a rerun of the read-modify-write cycle, the MC68000 will instead pe form the bus error exception processing routine, which we will describe late

BUS ARBITRATION LOGIC

The bus arbitration logic provided by the MC68000 is straightforwar The MC68000 does not prioritize requests for bus accesses by extern devices. The processor assumes that it is the lowest priority device in th system since it always grants bus access to any requesting device so long a the processor is not currently using the bus itself. Thus the MC68000 allow other devices to utilize the bus between instructions and between bus cycles a single instruction. Since there is no built-in arbitration there should be som external bus arbitration logic in a system of any complexity to prioritiz requests for the System Bus so that a high priority device is not superseded b low priority devices.

There are three signals associated with the bus arbitration logic: Bu Request ($\overline{\text{BR}}$), Bus Grant ($\overline{\text{BG}}$), and Bus Grant Acknowledge ($\overline{\text{BGACK}}$ When the MC68000 is using the System Bus without competition, the inpu

signals — $\overline{BR}$ and $\overline{BGACK}$ — will be inactive and the $\overline{BG}$ output will be negated.

Bus   Figure 3-10 illustrates the timing for the bus arbitration performed by
Arbitration **the MC68000. Bus arbitration commences when an external device pulls the**
Timing $\overline{BR}$ **input low.** When the MC68000 receives a bus request, it will respond by
asserting $\overline{BG}$ one CLK period later. The only exception to this immediate
response is when the MC68000 is in the initial stages of a bus cycle but has not
yet asserted $\overline{AS}$. In this case the MC68000 waits until one CLK period after $\overline{AS}$
has been asserted before it asserts $\overline{BG}$; the response time in this case will be a
maximum of three CLK periods.

Determining   Obviously, **the Bus Grant signal does not indicate that the bus is**
Bus   **available for use by the requesting device at that point — the MC68000 may**
Availability **still be using the bus to complete its current bus cycle. Therefore the device**

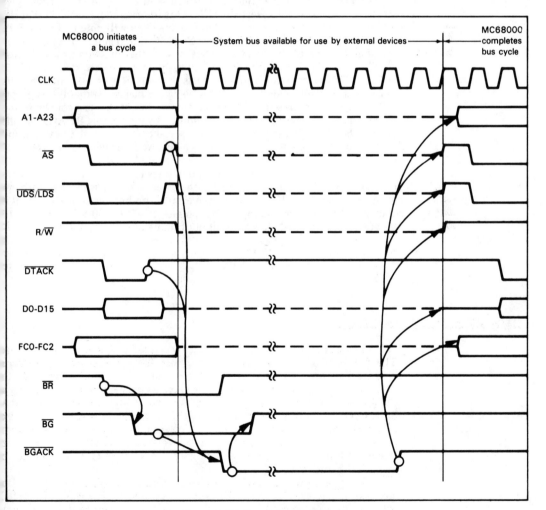

Figure 3-10. Bus Arbitration Timing

requesting the bus must monitor several other signals to determine when the bus is actually available for its use. First, the external device must wait until $\overline{AS}$ is negated, indicating that the MC68000 has completed the current bus cycle. The device requesting the bus must also wait until the $\overline{DTACK}$ signal is negated, since this indicates that the device involved in the current MC68000 cycle is no longer using the bus. However, in some systems it may not be necessary to monitor the $\overline{DTACK}$ signal. This is the case when system timing is such that you are always assured that all external devices will be off the bus when $\overline{AS}$ is negated. Lastly, the requesting device must check the state of the $\overline{BGACK}$ signal. If this signal is true, it indicates that some other device in the system has already been granted use of the System Bus and has not yet finished with it. Conversely, if $\overline{BGACK}$ is false, then the System Bus will be available for use at the end of the current cycle.

After all of the signal conditions we have described are met, the device requesting the bus must assert $\overline{BGACK}$. This informs the MC68000 that the requesting device has taken control of the bus. You will note in Figure 3-10 that the MC68000 does not wait for the $\overline{BGACK}$ signal before it relinquishes control of the bus: the Address and Data Busses, the Function Code outputs, $\overline{AS}$, $\overline{UDS}$, $\overline{LDS}$, and R/$\overline{W}$ are all placed in the high impedance state as soon as the MC68000 has completed the bus cycle that was in progress when the bus request was received. The device that is using the bus must hold $\overline{BGACK}$ low for as long as it requires the bus. While an external device has control of the bus, external logic should prevent bus conflicts by monitoring $\overline{BGACK}$; at this point the behavior of $\overline{BR}$ and $\overline{BC}$ is unimportant. However, the device using the bus should negate its $\overline{BR}$ before negating $\overline{BGACK}$ to avoid an incorrect bus request.

The MC68000 will maintain its output lines in the high impedance state until $\overline{BGACK}$ is negated, indicating that the external device is through with the bus. At that point the MC68000 is free to initiate another bus cycle. Note that if another bus request is pending at that point, the MC68000 will acquiesce to that bus request immediately without performing any bus cycles itself.

4

Exception Processing Logic

All of Motorola's literature on the MC68000 refers to "exception processing" when discussing what we usually describe as the interrupt system in other microprocessors. They have chosen to use this nomenclature since the events that can cause "interrupts" in the MC68000 cover a much broader range than those usually associated with an interrupt request in a typical microprocessor. We will also use the "exception processing" nomenclature.

The MC68000 provides exception processing logic. This logic is similar to that provided by the 8086 and Z8000 in that a jump vector table is used to transfer program control to the appropriate handler program whenever an exception occurs. The biggest difference between the MC68000's logic and that of the Z8000 and 8086 is that the number of events that can generate an exception in the MC68000 is greater than the number of events that cause interrupts in the Z8000. In addition, the MC68000 provides a 7-level priority structure for external interrupt requests.

Operating Modes
Before proceeding to describe the exception processing system, let us discuss the operating modes of the MC68000, since these affect exception processing. As we mentioned previously, the MC68000 can operate in either a Supervisor mode or a User mode. When the MC68000 is reset using the RESET input, it starts operating in the Supervisor mode. The processor remains in Supervisor mode until one of the following instructions is executed: Return from Exception (RTE), Move to Status Register (MOVE word to SR), AND Immediate to Status Register (ANDI word to SR), and Exclusive OR Immediate to Status Register (EORI word to SR). None of these instructions automatically causes the transition to the User mode of operation — rather, they are capable of changing the state of the S-bit in the Status register. If one of these instructions resets the S-bit, the MC68000 will begin operating in the User mode.

Once the MC68000 is operating in the User mode, the only thing that can cause a transition back to the Supervisor mode is an exception. All exception processing is performed in Supervisor mode regardless of the current setting of the S-bit of the Status register. When the exception processing has been completed, the Return from Exception (RTE) instruction allows return to the User mode.

A number of instructions, designated as "privileged," are reserved for the Supervisor mode. An attempt to execute one of these instructions in the User mode results in a "privilege violation" which is one type of exception. We will discuss these instructions and the privilege violation response later in this chapter.

EXCEPTION TYPES

Exceptions originate in a variety of ways which can be divided into two general categories:

1. **Internally generated exceptions** that result from the execution of certain instructions, or from internally detected errors.
2. **Externally generated exceptions** which include bus errors, reset, and interrupt requests.

The response of the MC68000 to the various types of exceptions is similar. Before we describe this response, let us look at the sources of exceptions since they go well beyond those provided by other microprocessors.

**Internally
Generated
Exceptions**
The internally generated exceptions to which the MC68000 responds can be further subdivided into three categories: internally detected errors, instruction traps, and the Trace function.

The following are the internally detected errors which will cause the MC68000 to initiate exception processing:

1. **Addressing errors.** Whenever the MC68000 attempts to access word data, long word data, or an instruction at an odd address, this is an address error since all such accesses must be on even address boundaries.
2. **Privilege violations.** Again, some instructions are reserved for use only in the Supervisor mode. Exception processing will be initiated if you attempt to execute any of the following instructions when in the User mode: STOP, RESET, RTE, MOVE to SR, AND (word) Immediate to SR, EOR (word) Immediate to SR, OR (word) Immediate to SR, MOVE USP.
3. **Illegal and unimplemented opcodes.** If an instruction is fetched whose bit pattern is not one of the defined instruction bit patterns for the MC68000, exception processing will be initiated. Two bit patterns are defined as unimplemented rather than illegal; if bits 15-12 are 1010 or 1111, these are treated as unimplemented instruction opcodes. If these opcodes are fetched, special exception processing is initiated which can allow you to use these unimplemented instructions in your own software.

Instruction traps are exceptions which are caused by the execution of instructions in your program. There is a standard TRAP instruction which is similar to the Z8000 System Call instruction. **There are four other instructions — TRAPV, CHK, DIVS, and DIVU — which will cause exception**

processing to be initiated if certain conditions, such as arithmetic overflows or divide by zero, are detected.

The third type of internally generated exception occurs when the MC68000 is operating with the Trace function. If the T-bit in the supervisor portion of the Status register is set, exception processing will be performed after each instruction. The Trace function is used for program debugging since you can analyze, by stepping through the program, the results of each instruction's execution.

Externally Generated Exceptions

There are three different types of externally generated exceptions:

1. **Bus errors.** When the $\overline{BERR}$ signal is pulled low by external logic (while $\overline{HALT}$ is high) exception processing is initiated.

2. **Reset.** When the $\overline{RESET}$ signal is asserted by external logic, exception processing is initiated.

3. **Interrupt request.** This is the most familiar form of exception processing and is initiated by external logic via the three interrupt request lines ($\overline{IPL0}$, $\overline{IPL1}$, and $\overline{IPL2}$).

Exception Priorities

The different types of exceptions have different priorities, and processing of an exception depends on its priority. The following table lists the types of exceptions according to their relative priorities, and also defines when processing of each type begins.

Priority	Exception Source	Exception Processing Response
Highest	$\overline{RESET}$ $\overline{BERR}$ (Bus Error) Address Error	Abort current cycle, then process exception
	Trace Interrupt Request Illegal/Unimplemented Opcode Privilege Violation	Complete current instruction, then process exception
Lowest	TRAP, TRAPV CHK Divide-by-zero	Instruction execution initiates exception processing

The highest priority types of exceptions are Reset, Bus Error, and Address Error. Any of these exceptions will cause immediate termination of the current instruction, even within a bus cycle. The next group of exceptions — trace, interrupt requests, illegal/unimplemented instructions, and privilege violations — allow completion of the current instruction before initiating exception processing. Note that interrupt requests include an additional prioritization which we discussed earlier. The lowest priority of exceptions are those that are caused by trap-type instructions. These instructions can initiate exception processing as part of their normal execution. All of the instruction trap exceptions have equal priority since it is impossible for two of them to generate exceptions simultaneously.

Exception Vector Table

Central to the MC68000 exception processing sequence is a vector table that occupies 1024 bytes (512 sixteen-bit words) of memory. This table occupies memory addresses 000000_{16} through $0003FF_{16}$. Figure 4-1 illustrates the exception vector table. The table is organized as 256 four-byte vectors. Each vector is a 32-bit address which will be loaded into the Program Counter as part of the exception processing sequence.

As you can see, a number of the vector table entries serve the defined

Memory Addresses (Hex)	16 Bits	
000000	SSP (High)	Reset - Initial SSP
000002	SSP (Low)	
000004	PC0 (High)	Reset - Initial PC
000006	PC0 (Low)	
000008	PC2 (High)	Vector 2 - Bus Error
00000A	PC2 (Low)	
00000C	PC3 (High)	Vector 3 - Address Error
00000E	PC3 (Low)	
000010	PC4 (High)	Vector 4 - Illegal Instruction
000012	PC4 (Low)	
000014	PC5 (High)	Vector 5 - Divide by 0
000016	PC5 (Low)	
000018	PC6 (High)	Vector 6 - CHK Instruction
00001A	PC6 (Low)	
00001C	PC7 (High)	Vector 7 - TRAPV Instruction
00001E	PC7 (Low)	
000020	PC8 (High)	Vector 8 - Privilege Violation
000022	PC8 (Low)	
000024	PC9 (High)	Vector 9 - Trace
000026	PC9 (Low)	
000028	PC10 (High)	Vector 10_{10} - Opcode 1010 Emulation
00002A	PC10 (Low)	
00002C	PC11 (High)	Vector 11_{10} - Opcode 1111 Emulation
00002E	PC11 (Low)	
000030	PC12 (High)	Vector 12_{10}
000032	PC12 (Low)	
		Reserved by Motorola
00005C	PC23 (High)	Vector 23_{10}
00005E	PC23 (Low)	
000060	PC24 (High)	Vector 24_{10} - Spurious Interrupt
000062	PC24 (Low)	
000064	PC25 (High)	Vector 25_{10} - Level 1 Interrupt
000066	PC25 (Low)	
000068	PC26 (High)	Vector 26_{10} - Level 2 Interrupt
00006A	PC26 (Low)	
00006C	PC27 (High)	Vector 27_{10} - Level 3 Interrupt
00006E	PC27 (Low)	
000070	PC28 (High)	Vector 28_{10} - Level 4 Interrupt
000072	PC28 (Low)	
000074	PC29 (High)	Vector 29_{10} - Level 5 Interrupt
000076	PC29 (Low)	
000078	PC30 (High)	Vector 30_{10} - Level 6 Interrupt
00007A	PC30 (Low)	
00007C	PC31 (High)	Vector 31_{10} - Level 7 Interrupt
00007E	PC31 (Low)	
000080	PC32 (High)	Vector 32_{10}
000082	PC32 (Low)	
		TRAP Instruction Vectors
0000BC	PC47 (High)	Vector 47_{10}
0000BE	PC47 (Low)	
0000C0	PC48 (High)	Vector 48_{10}
0000C2	PC48 (Low)	
		Reserved by Motorola
0000FC	PC63 (High)	Vector 63
0000FE	PC63 (Low)	
000100	PC64 (High)	Vector 64
000102	PC64 (Low)	
		User Vectors
0003FC	PC255 (High)	Vector 255
0003FE	PC255 (Low)	

Auto-Vectors if $\overline{\text{VPA}}$ low

Figure 4-1. Exception Vector Table

types of exceptions which we have discussed. The remaining entries of the vector table are reserved for use by Motorola and should not be used by your program if compatibility with Motorola software is desired. The first 64 exception vectors have predefined uses; this leaves 192 vectors available to external interrupt requests — this should be more than enough for most applications. However, the first 64 vector locations are not protected by the MC68000; thus they can be used by external interrupts if a system requires it.

EXCEPTION PROCESSING SEQUENCES

The general sequence of events performed by the MC68000 in response to an exception is the same regardless of the source of the exception. There are, however, some differences. Let us begin by examining the response to internally generated exceptions.

Internally Generated Exception Processing

If exception processing is initiated as a result of either the Trace function, a TRAP instruction, an illegal or unimplemented opcode, or a privilege violation, the following steps occur:

1. The Status Register contents are copied into an internal register.
2. The S-bit in the Status Register is set, thus placing the MC68000 in the Supervisor mode of operation.
3. The T-bit in the Status Register is reset to disable tracing to allow for continuous execution when debugging using TRACE.
4. The Program Counter contents are pushed onto the Supervisor stack. The contents of SSP will be decremented by four since four bytes are required to store the 32-bit contents of PC.
5. Status register contents are pushed onto the Supervisor stack; SSP contents are decremented by two, since the Status register is a 16-bit register.
6. The new Program Counter contents are taken from the appropriate location in the interrupt vector table.
7. Instruction execution then begins at the location indicated by the new contents of the Program Counter; this will be the first instruction of the exception processing program you have provided for that particular type of exception.

Bus and Address Error Exception Processing

The way in which the MC68000 responds to an exception caused by a bus error or address error includes several steps in addition to those described in the preceding paragraphs. First, recall that either of these errors causes immediate termination of the bus cycle in progress. The next steps are the following:

1. The contents of the Status register are copied into an internal register.
2. The S-bit in the Status register is set, placing the MC68000 in the Supervisor mode.
3. The T-bit in the Status register is reset to disable trace operations.
4. The contents of the Program Counter are pushed onto the Supervisor stack and the System Stack Pointer (SSP) is decremented by four.
5. The contents of the Status register are pushed onto the Supervisor stack and the contents of SSP are decremented by two.

6. The contents of the MC68000's instruction register, which constitute the first word of the instruction that was in progress when the bus error occurred, are pushed onto the Supervisor stack and SSP is decremented by two.

7. The 32-bit address that was being used for the bus cycle which was terminated is also pushed onto the Supervisor stack and SSP is decremented by four.

8. A word which provides information as to the type of cycle that was in progress at the time of the error is pushed onto the Supervisor stack and SSP is decremented by two.

9. The Program Counter contents are taken from the appropriate interrupt vector — either the bus error vector or address error vector of the exception vector table.

10. Instruction execution resumes at the location indicated by the new contents of the Program Counter.

Figure 4-2 shows the order in which information is pushed onto the Supervisor stack as part of the exception processing for bus and address errors. The value saved for the Program Counter is advanced two to ten bytes beyond the address of the first word of the instruction where the error occurred according to the length of that instruction and its addressing information, if any.

As you can see in Figure 4-2, **the five least significant bits of the last word pushed onto the Stack provide information as to the type of access that was in progress when the bus error or address error occurred.** The three least significant bits are a copy of the Function Code outputs during the aborted bus cycle. Bit 3 indicates the type of processing that was in progress when the error occurred. This bit is set for Group 0 or 1 exception processing and reset for Group 2 exception and normal instruction processing. Bit 4 indicates whether a

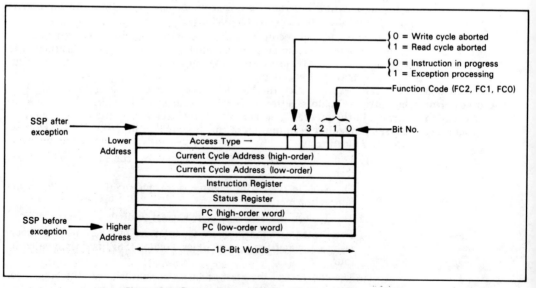

Figure 4-2. System Stack After Bus Error or Address Error

read (bit 4 set) or write (bit 4 reset) cycle was in progress when the error occurred. If an error occurs during the exception processing of a preceding bus error, address error, or reset operation, the MC68000 will enter the Halt state and remain there.

All of the information that is pushed onto the Supervisor stack as part of the bus and address error exception processing sequence is intended to aid you in analyzing possible sources of the error. Either of these errors implies a serious system failure and it is not likely that you will be able to return to normal program execution.

Reset Exception Processing

An external reset causes a special type of exception processing. After the RESET input has been pulsed low the following steps occur:

1. The S-bit in the Status register is set, placing the MC68000 in the Supervisor mode.
2. The T-bit in the Status register is reset to disable the Trace function.
3. All three interrupt mask bits in the Status register are set, thus specifying the interrupt priority mask at level seven.
4. The Supervisor Stack Pointer (SSP) is loaded with the contents of the first four bytes of memory (addresses 000000-000003).
5. The Program Counter (PC) is loaded from the next four bytes of memory (addresses 000004-000007).
6. Instruction execution commences at the address indicated by the new contents of the Program Counter, which should reference your power-up/reset initialization program.

Interrupt Request Exception Processing

The last type of exception processing we will discuss is the sequence initiated by the standard interrupt request. An external device requests an interrupt by encoding an interrupt request level on the IPL0-IPL2 inputs. The MC68000 compares these inputs to the interrupt mask bits in the Status register. If the encoded priority level is less than or equal to the one specified by the three-bit mask, the interrupt request will not be recognized by the MC68000. **If the encoded interrupt level is a higher priority than the level established by the interrupt mask (or if a level seven interrupt request is input) then the interrupt will be processed.** The MC68000 responds to the allowed interrupt request as soon as it completes the instruction execution currently in progress. **Upon completion of the current instruction, the following steps occur:**

1. The contents of the Status register are saved internally.
2. The S-bit in the Status register is set, placing the MC68000 in the Supervisor mode.
3. The T-bit in the Status register is reset to disable the Trace function.
4. The interrupt mask bits in the Status register are updated to the level of the interrupt request that is encoded on the IPL0-IPL2 inputs. This allows the current interrupt to be processed without being interrupted by lower priority events.
5. The MC68000 then performs an interrupt acknowledge bus cycle. This cycle serves two functions; first, the processor lets the requesting device know that its interrupt request is being serviced, and second, the processor fetches an exception vector byte from the requesting device. **Figure 4-3 shows the timing for this interrupt acknowledge/ vector fetch cycle. This cycle is essentially a read cycle with a few minor differences.** First, address lines A1 through A3 will reflect the states of the IPL0-IPL2 inputs so that external logic can determine

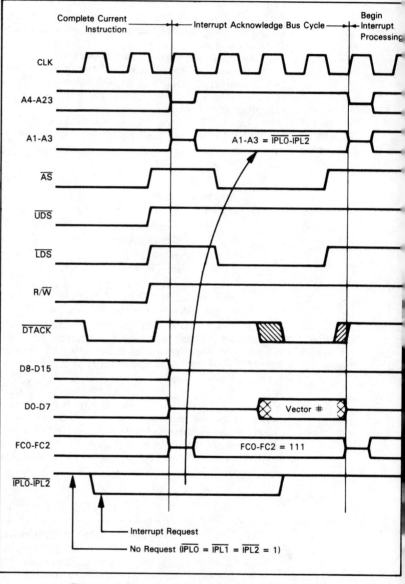

Figure 4-3. Interrupt Acknowledge/Vector Fetch Cycle

which interrupt request is being processed. All of the other address
outputs are set during the interrupt acknowledge cycle. The requesting device responds to the MC68000 by placing a byte of exception
vector data on the lower half of the Data Bus. The Data Transfer
Acknowledge ($\overline{\text{DTACK}}$) signal is used to effect this transfer of data
just as with a normal read cycle. Throughout the interrupt
acknowledge cycle, the Function Code outputs (FC0-FC2) will be set

high since this represents the interrupt acknowledge function code. After the vector byte has been read from the interrupting device, the MC68000 proceeds with the following exception processing steps.

6. The contents of the Program Counter are pushed onto the Supervisor stack and SSP is decremented by four.

7. The contents of the Status register are pushed onto the Supervisor stack and SSP is decremented by two.

8. The Program Counter is loaded with four bytes of data from the appropriate location in the exception vector table. The address for this location is derived as shown in the following illustration:

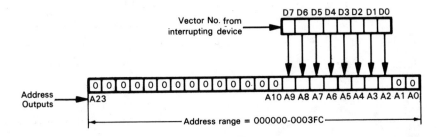

The eight bits of data that were read from the requesting device as part of the interrupt acknowledge cycle are used to form address bits A2 through A9. The two least significant bits and bits A10 through A23 will all be set to zero. Thus, addresses 000000_{16} through $0003FC_{16}$ can be generated. If you refer to Figure 4-1, you will see that these are the upper and lower boundaries of the exception vector table. Under normal circumstances a requesting device should limit itself to producing vectors corresponding to the address range $0000FC_{16}$ through $0003FC_{16}$ since the lower addresses in the vector table have preassigned uses.

After the Program Counter has been loaded with the new value from the exception vector table, instruction execution commences at the location indicated by the new contents of the Program Counter; this will be the first instruction of your interrupt processing routine for the particular device requesting the interrupt.

Spurious Interrupt

There are two variations to the interrupt request processing sequence we have just described. First, if during the interrupt acknowledge bus cycle the requesting device responds by asserting BERR instead of DTACK, the MC68000 treats this as an indication that the current interrupt request is a spurious one, and it will use vector 24 in the exception vector table to load the Program Counter.

Autovector Interrupt Response

The second variation on interrupt request processing is the autovector response. If you refer to Figure 4-1, you will see that seven vector locations are provided in the exception vector table for autovectors, corresponding to the seven interrupt priority levels. These vectors will be used if the device requesting an interrupt responds to the interrupt acknowledge bus cycle by asserting the Valid Peripheral Address (VPA) signal instead of supplying a byte of vector data. If this occurs, the MC68000 will respond by asserting the Valid Memory Address (VMA) signal. The processor will then use the appropriate autovector from the exception vector table to obtain a new Program Counter value. This autovector response was provided specifically to emulate the interrupt timing sequence expected by 6800-family periphera devices. The $\overline{VPA}/\overline{VMA}$ sequence is the standard 6800 microprocessor interrupt sequence. Of course a non-6800-family device in the system could also exploit this autovector capability should it be advantageous.

5

Addressing Modes

The MC68000 utilizes 14 different addressing modes which can be grouped into six basic types. These are:

1. **Direct Register Addressing**
   a. Data Register Direct
   b. Address Register Direct
2. **Direct Memory Addressing**
   a. Absolute Short
   b. Absolute Long
3. **Indirect Memory Addressing**
   a. Register Indirect
   b. Post-increment Register Indirect
   c. Pre-decrement Register Indirect
   d. Register Indirect with Displacement
   e. Register Indirect with Index and Displacement
4. **Implied Register Addressing**
5. **Program Counter Relative Addressing**
   a. PC-relative with Displacement
   b. PC-relative with Index and Displacement
6. **Immediate Data Addressing**
   a. Immediate
   b. Quick Immediate

These addressing modes help create a powerful and efficient instruction set. In particular, two useful features of the MC68000 addressing are that any address register may be used for direct or indirect addressing, and any register may be used as an index register.

The general format of a single effective address instruction operation word is shown below. The two least significant 3-bit fields determine the effective address. These fields are the mode field (bits 3-5) and the register field (bits 0-2).

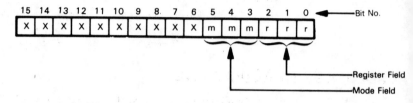

Effective Address Extension

In some cases, the information contained in these two fields may be appended to fully specify the operand. In this case, **one or two additional words are appended onto the instruction**. This additional information is called the effective address extension, and its format is:

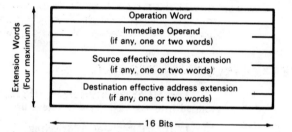

We will now discuss the addressing modes in detail. The following abbreviations are used within this section.

An	Address register n ($0 \le n \le 7$)
CCR	Condition code half of the Status register
dddd	Displacement value
Dn	Data register n ($0 \le n \le 7$)
EA	Effective address
N	Operand size in bytes (1, 2, or 4)
PC	Program Counter
pppp qqqq xxxx yyyy zzzz	Any four hex digits
Rn	Any address or data register n ($0 \le n \le 7$)
rrr	The 3-bit value of n
SP	The active Stack Pointer
SR	Status register
SSP	Supervisor Stack Pointer
ssss	Sign extension digits
USP	User Stack Pointer

REGISTER DIRECT ADDRESSING

This addressing mode requires that the operand involved be contained in one of the eight Data registers or one of the eight Address registers (Mode = 001_2).

Data Register Direct	Address Register Direct
EA = Dn	EA = An
Mode = 000_2	Mode = 001_2

ABSOLUTE DATA ADDRESSING

There are two forms of this addressing mode. The short form is called absolute short addressing, while the longer format is called absolute long.

Absolute Short **Absolute short.** One extension word is necessary for this addressing mode. The address of the operand is the sign extended value of the extension word. Figure 5-1 illustrates the absolute short addressing mode.

Absolute Long **Absolute long.** Two words of extension are required for this addressing mode. The address of the operand is the concatenation of the two extension words; the first is the high-order portion, the second is the low-order portion. Figure 5-2 illustrates the absolute long addressing mode.

REGISTER INDIRECT ADDRESSING

Each of the five variations of this addressing mode reference an operand in memory.

Address Register Indirect **Address register indirect.** In this mode, the address of the operand is the contents of the specified Address register. Figure 5-3 illustrates the Address register indirect mode.

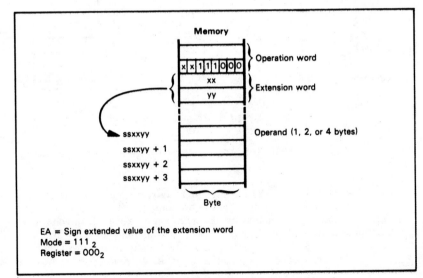

Figure 5-1. Absolute Short Direct Memory Addressing

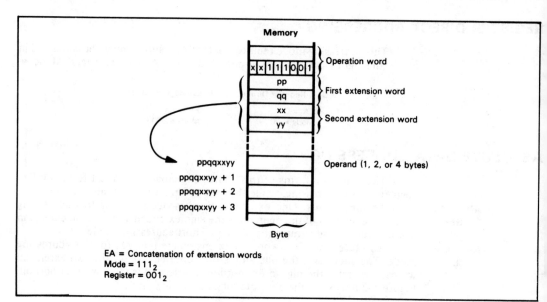

Figure 5-2. Absolute Long Direct Memory Addressing

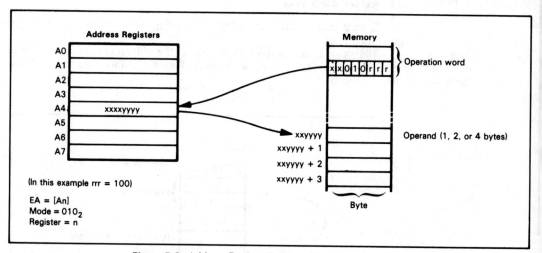

Figure 5-3. Address Register Indirect Memory Addressing

Register Indirect with Postincrement

Address register indirect with postincrement. In this mode, the address of the operand is the contents of the specified Address register. After the instruction using this mode is executed, the contents of this register are incremented by one, two, or four depending on the size of the operand. If the Address register is A7 (SP) then the address is incremented by two regardless of the operand size, because the Stack Pointer must be kept on a word boundary. Figure 5-4 illustrates the Address register indirect with postincrement mode.

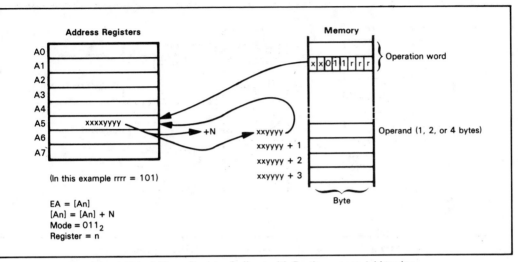

Figure 5-4. Address Register Indirect with Postincrement Addressing

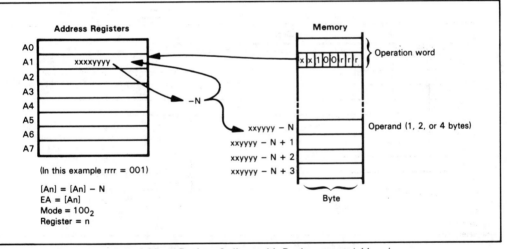

Figure 5-5. Address Register Indirect with Predecrement Addressing

Register Indirect with Predecrement

Address register indirect with predecrement. This addressing mode is similar to the previous one with the exception that the contents of the specified Address register are decremented before they are used to reference the operand. Again, if A7 is specified then the address is always decremented by two. Figure 5-5 illustrates the Address register indirect with predecrement mode.

Register Indirect with Displacement

Address register indirect with displacement. One word of extension is required with this addressing mode. The address of the operand is the sum of the contents of the specified Address register and the sign-extended 16-bit displacement word contained in the extension word. Figure 5-6 illustrates the Address register indirect with displacement mode.

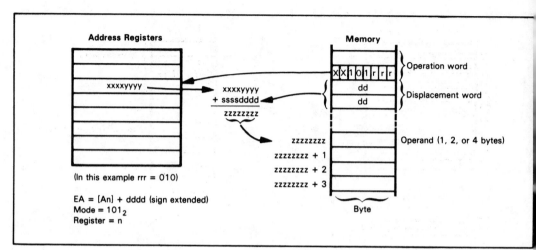

Figure 5-6. Address Register Indirect with Displacement Addressing

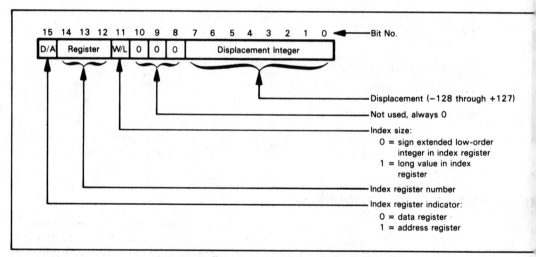

Figure 5-7. Extension Word Format for Indexing

Indexed Register Indirect

Address register indirect with index and displacement. This addressing mode requires one word of extension which is formatted as shown in Figure 5-7. The operand address is the sum of the specified Address register, the sign-extend displacement integer in the least significant byte of the extension word, and the contents of the Index register. Address formation for the Address register indirect with index and displacement mode is illustrated in Figure 5-8.

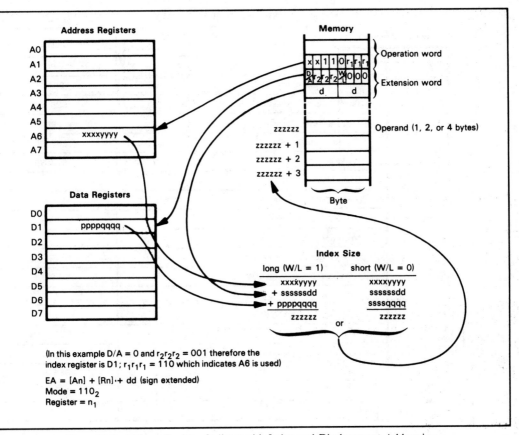

Figure 5-8. Address Register Indirect with Index and Displacement Addressing

IMPLIED REGISTER ADDRESSING

There are some instructions that implicitly refer to a specific register. These registers are the Program Counter (PC), the Stack Pointer (SP-SSP or USP), and the Status register (SR). Table 5-1 shows those instructions in which a register holding the operand is implied.

PROGRAM COUNTER RELATIVE ADDRESSING

There are two formats for PC-relative addressing. Both require one word of extension and both provide displacement. The second format includes indexing in addition to displacement.

The value contained in the Program Counter which is used in address calculation is the address of the extension word.

Table 5-1. MC68000 Instructions Which Use Implied Registers

Instruction	Implied Register(s)
Branch Conditional (Bcc), Branch Always (BRA)	PC
Branch to Subroutine (BSR)	PC, SP
Check Register against Bounds (CHK)	SSP, SR
Test Condition, Decrement and Branch (DBcc)	PC
Signed Divide (DIVS)	SSP, SR
Unsigned Divide (DIVU)	SSP, SR
Jump (JMP)	PC
Jump to Subroutine (JSR)	PC, SP
Link and Allocate (LINK)	SP
Move Condition Codes (MOVE CCR)	SR
Move Status Register (MOVE SR)	SR
Move User Stack Pointer (MOVE USP)	USP
Push Effective Address (PEA)	SP
Return from Exception (RTE)	PC, SP, SR
Return and Restore Condition Codes (RTR)	PC, SP, SR
Return from Subroutine (RTS)	PC, SP
Trap (TRAP)	SSP, SR
Trap on Overflow (TRAPV)	SSP, SR
Unlink (UNLK)	SP

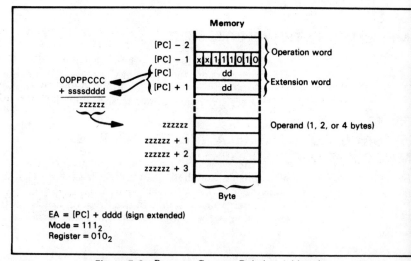

Figure 5-9. Program Counter-Relative Addressing

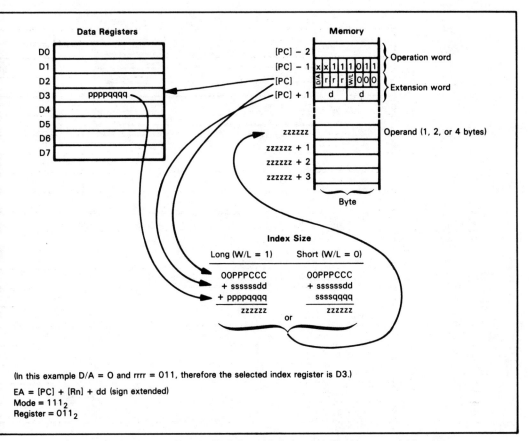

Figure 5-10. Program Counter-Relative with Index and Displacement Addressing

PC-relative
with
Displacement

PC-relative with displacement. This addressing mode generates an effective address by summing together the value of the Program Counter and the sign extended value of the extension word. Figure 5-9 illustrates the PC-relative with displacement mode.

PC-relative
Indexed

PC-relative with index and displacement. This mode requires an extension word format similar to that required by the Address register indirect with index and displacement mode (see Figure 5-7). The address is calculated as shown in Figure 5-10.

IMMEDIATE DATA ADDRESSING

The operand for immediate data addressing is the value that immediately follows the instruction word. Thus, depending on the size of the operand, either one or two extension words will be necessary, as illustrated in Figure 5-11.

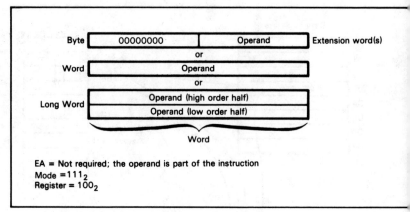

Figure 5-11. MC68000 Immediate Data Addressing Extension Words

6

The Instruction Set

Instruction
Summary
Tables Table A-2 in Appendix A summarizes the instruction set of the MC68000. Instruction object codes and execution times are given alphabetically in Table B-1. Instruction object codes are given numerically in Table C-1.

When compared to other microprocessor instruction sets, the MC68000 instruction set might seem quite large: over 300 instructions are listed in Table A-2. However, if you examine this table closely, you will see that slight variations of the same instruction mnemonic may appear several times. These are different forms of the same instruction. **There are actually 56 basic instructions provided in the MC68000.** We have listed all the variations of a single instruction as though they were distinct instructions in order to make our description of the instruction set consistent with similar ones for other microprocessors.

One of the most significant characteristics of the MC68000 instruction set is its orderliness. Despite its apparent complexity, this instruction set should be relatively easy to learn, since the variations are consistent and therefore predictable. These variations are due to the different addressing modes available and to the MC68000's ability to handle five different data types. Since there are really only 56 basic mnemonics that you must learn, it is more likely that you will use all of the instructions in the way that they were intended and thus obtain the full power of the instruction set.

Let us examine the MC68000 instruction set by instruction categories, as given in Table A-2.

One thing to keep in mind is that the MC68000 uses memory-mapped I/O: therefore there are no separate I/O instructions. The primary memory reference instructions will also be used to accomplish I/O.

The basic format of all instructions is the same. The op-code for every instruction is one word. Additional extension words are required when the addressing modes specified use constants (immediate operands), absolute addresses, or displacements. Accordingly, **an instruction can be anywhere from 2 to 10 bytes in length. The number of bytes for each instruction is listed in Table A-2.**

Memory Reference Instructions

All of the primary memory reference instructions have byte, word, and long word versions. Secondary memory reference instructions can use most of the memory addressing modes. There are byte, word, and long word versions of most, but not all, of these instructions.

Move Instructions

The Move instruction provided by the MC68000 allows data movement between registers, from register to memory, from memory to register, and directly from one memory location to another. The Move Multiple Register (MOVEM) instruction allows all of the MC68000 register contents to be quickly saved in memory or restored from memory.

The MC68000 does not provide a block move instruction such as those available with the 8086 and the Z8000 microprocessors. However, since the Move instructions can move data from one memory location to another, **it is simple to move blocks of data by using the Move instruction in conjunction with the Decrement and Branch (DBcc) instruction.**

Multiply and Divide Instructions

Both signed and unsigned multiply and divide instructions are included in the instruction set. In comparison, the Z8000 provided only unsigned multiplication and division. However, the Z8000 provides 32-bit multiplication and division while the MC68000 can only multiply two 16-bit operands producing a 32-bit result, or divide a 32-bit dividend by a 16-bit divisor. **The divide instructions reference the dividend in one of the Data registers: the divisor may reside in memory or in another Data register. Both** the divisor and the dividend are treated as signed binary numbers in the DIVS instruction and as unsigned binary numbers in the DIVU instruction. After the division instruction has been executed, the quotient is returned in the low order half of the dividend register and the remainder is returned in the high order half of the dividend register.

The multiply instructions also have only a word version; there is no long word version. As with division, there is a signed (MULS) and unsigned (MULU) version of the multiply instructions. One of the operands must reside in the least significant half of a Data register while the other operand can be either a memory word, the lower half of another Data register, or can consist of immediate data included as part of the instruction. Upon completion of the multiply operation, the 32-bit product is returned in the source operand Data register.

Jump and Branch Instructions

The MC68000 includes standard Jump and Jump to Subroutine instructions (JMP and JSR) which use specific addresses for loading the Program Counter. **There are also the Branch Always and Branch to Subroutine instructions (BRA and BSR)** which cause a transfer of program control relative to the Program Counter's current contents.

The Trap instruction is the MC68000's equivalent of the System Call instruction provided by the Z8000. You will recall from the earlier discussion of the MC68000 exception processing logic that the Trap instruction automatically switches the MC68000 into the Supervisor mode, which utilizes a separate Stack Pointer to isolate the operating system from application programs.

The MC68000 also provides several instructions that are specifically designed to simplify implementation of higher level languages. These instructions are unique to the MC68000. The Link (LINK) and Unlink (UNLK) instructions can be used to maintain a linked list of local data and

parameter areas on the Stack and thus simplify operations where there are frequent interrupts of nested subroutines.

Link and Unlink Instructions

The Link instruction uses the System Stack Pointer (SFP), one of the other Address registers, as a "Frame Pointer" and a displacement value. This instruction will typically be used at the beginning of a subroutine. The Link instruction first pushes the current value of the Frame Pointer onto the Stack. The current value of the Stack Pointer is then loaded into the Frame Pointer so that it now points to the top of the current Stack. Finally, the displacement value included with the Link instruction is used to decrement the System Stack Pointer so that it is displaced to clear a space in memory for storage of such things as local variables and parameters. These variables can then be accessed via the Frame Pointer. The Unlink (UNLK) instruction is used to clean up the Stack at the end of a subroutine and would be executed just prior to returning to a higher level subroutine. The Unlink instruction loads the System Stack Pointer with the contents of the Frame Pointer. The Frame Pointer is then loaded with the address pulled off the Stack. Thus, both the Frame Pointer and the System Stack Pointer will be restored to the values they held before the subroutine was called.

Interfacing the MC68000 with 6800 Peripherals

Many peripheral components have been developed by Motorola and other manufacturers for the 8-bit 6800 microprocessor. In general, any asynchronous peripheral device can be used with the MC68000 with only a small amount of external logic needed to meet the interface requirements (handshaking, etc.). However, the 6800-family components are based on synchronous read/write operations. This imposes certain constraints when you attempt to use a 6800 peripheral device with an asynchronous processor such as the MC68000. Obviously, it was in Motorola's interest to design the MC68000 so that it would be able to use both conventional asynchronous devices and the family of existing synchronous 6800 devices. Therefore they have included logic to simplify interfacing 6800 peripheral devices.

Again, the MC68000 performs read/write operations asynchronously. The signals involved with these operations are the strobes ($\overline{AS}$, $\overline{UDS}$, $\overline{LDS}$), the R/$\overline{W}$ signal, the Data Transfer Acknowledge signal ($\overline{DTACK}$), and of course the address (A1-A23) and data (D0-D15) signals.

6800 Peripheral Signals   Three additional signals are used to perform the synchronous read/write operations required by 6800 peripheral devices. These signals are Valid Memory Address ($\overline{VMA}$), Valid Peripheral Address ($\overline{VPA}$), and Enable (E). Figure 7-1 illustrates the timing of the synchronous read and write cycles. After the MC68000 has output the address on A1-A23 and has asserted the Address Strobe ($\overline{AS}$), external logic is expected to decode information on the address lines. If a 6800 peripheral device is being addressed, then the external logic should assert the $\overline{VPA}$ input to the MC68000. This causes the MC68000 to emulate the data transfer timing of the 6800 microprocessor. As a result, the transfer of data is synchronized with the clock signal E. The MC68000 will keep the address outputs valid throughout this cycle.

During a read cycle, the 6800 peripheral device is expected to place data on the Data Bus when the E signal is high. Note that the Data Transfer

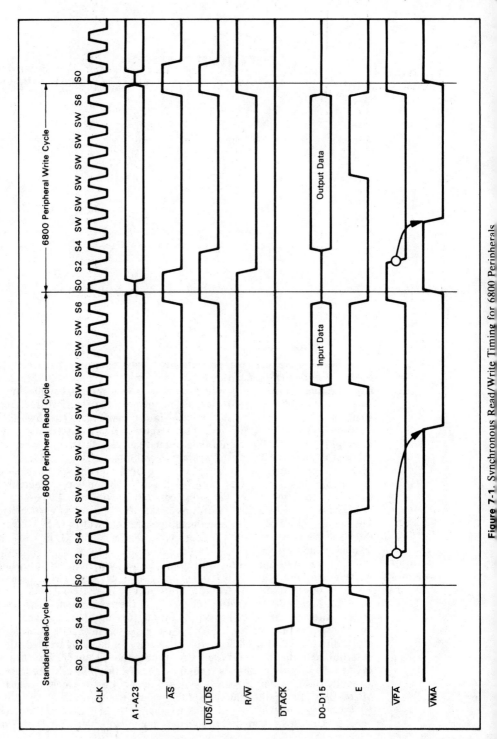

Figure 7-1. Synchronous Read/Write Timing for 6800 Peripherals

Acknowledge ($\overline{\text{DTACK}}$) signal is not used since that signal implies an asynchronous transfer of data. Instead, the falling edge of E indicates that the data transfer (either read or write) has been completed. The MC68000 then proceeds to complete the cycle in the normal fashion by negating the strobe signals and returning the Address Bus to the high impedance state.

6800
Read/Write
Timing

You will note in Figure 7-1 that there is a difference in the total number of CLK cycles for the read and write operations. You should not infer from this that all 6800-type read operations take four more CLK cycles than write operations. That is only the case in the example shown, and has to do with the phase of E when the read or write operation was begun. In general, the E signal and the current MC68000 cycle state will not be synchronized at the outset of a 6800 reference cycle. This is because the E signal has a duty cycle of 40%: E is high for four CLK periods and low for six CLK periods. The MC68000 instruction cycles, on the other hand, vary in the number of CLK signal periods needed to execute. During the write cycle we have shown in Figure 7-1, the E signal is in synchronization with the instruction execution cycle. Thus this particular write cycle takes the minimum possible number of CLK cycles to execute. Note that the MC68000 automatically inserts Wait states after the $\overline{\text{VPA}}$ signal is input. The number of Wait states inserted will depend on how much time is needed in order to synchronize with the signal.

The $\overline{\text{VMA}}$ signal is output by the MC68000 in response to the $\overline{\text{VPA}}$ output.

At the end of the read or write cycle, the 6800 peripheral device or the address decoding logic in the system must negate the $\overline{\text{VPA}}$ signal within one clock period after the MC68000 negates $\overline{\text{AS}}$. Otherwise, the MC68000 will assume that the following cycle is also supposed to be a 6800-type synchronous cycle.

Figure 7-2 summarizes the timing constraints of 6800 peripherals. It includes the 6800 processor signals for reference so you can compare them with those associated with the MC68000.

A SIMPLE MC68000/6800 INTERFACE EXAMPLE

Figure 7-3 illustrates a simple interface of two 6800 peripheral devices in an MC68000-based system. In this example, the address region 000000_{16} through $7FFFFF_{16}$ (the lower eight megabytes) is used for asynchronous devices including memory. The upper eight megabytes is used, albeit inefficiently, for the two synchronous 6800 peripheral devices. The PIA (Peripheral Interface Adapter) is assigned addresses 800000_{16} through $BFFFFF_{16}$, while the ACIA (Asynchronous Communications Interface Adapter) is assigned addresses $C00000_{16}$ through $FFFFFF_{16}$.

Interrupt request signals are connected directly to the $\overline{\text{IPL0}}$ and $\overline{\text{IPL1}}$ input pins of the MC68000. Note that $\overline{\text{IPL2}}$ is tied high. In this example, an interrupt from the ACIA causes $\overline{\text{IPL0}}$ to become active thus generating an interrupt of level 1 (the lowest priority). Both PIA interrupts are connected to $\overline{\text{IPL1}}$. When either of these becomes active, an interrupt of level 2 is generated. If both the ACIA and the PIA request an interrupt simultaneously, an interrupt of level 3 would be generated.

For a detailed description of how the MC68000 responds to interrupt requests, refer to our earlier discussion of MC68000 exception processing in Chapter 4.

We have also included logic that will cause the MC68000 to use its

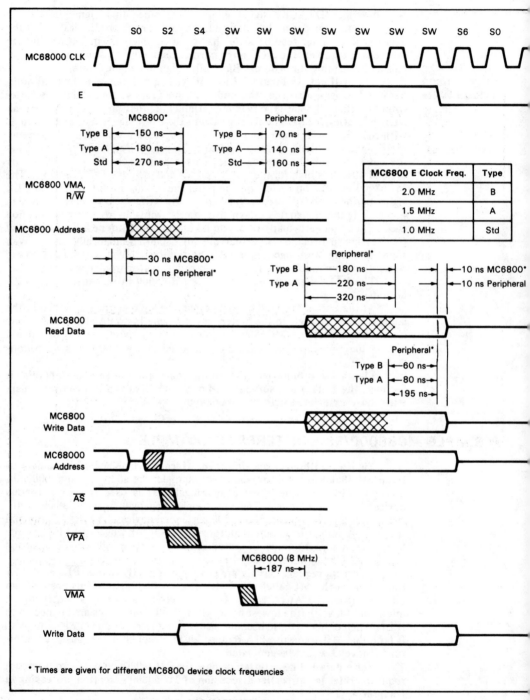

Figure 7-2. MC68000/6800 Interface Timing Signal Summary

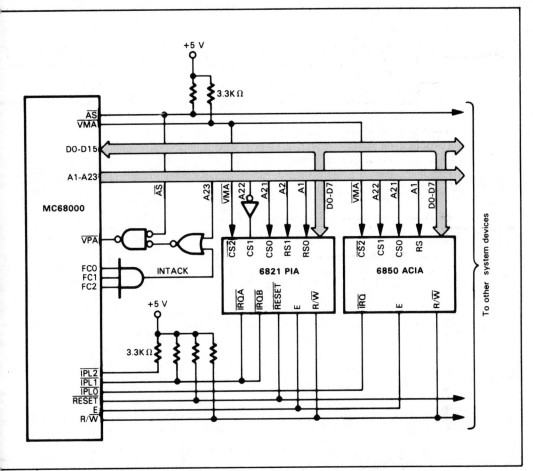

Figure 7-3. A Simple MC68000/6800 Interface Example

autovector capability during response to an interrupt request from one of the 6800 family devices. Recall that if the $\overline{VPA}$ signal is asserted to the MC68000 during an interrupt acknowledge cycle, then no byte of vector data need be supplied by the requesting device; instead, the MC68000 gets the appropriate autovector from the exception processing vector table.

A

The Instruction Set Summary

Table A-2 summarizes the MC68000 instruction set. The MNEMONIC column lists the instruction mnemonic (e.g., MOVE, ADD, JMP). The OPERAND(S) column lists the operands used with the instruction mnemonic.

The fixed part of an assembly language instruction is shown in UPPER CASE. The variable part (register number, address, immediate data, etc.) is shown in lower case.

The BYTES and CLOCK CYCLES are repeated in this table for reader convenience. Refer to Appendix B for a description of these entries.

ALTERNATE MNEMONICS

The MC68000 instruction set allows a choice of mnemonics for many operations. An "I" can be appended to the instruction mnemonic for an immediate operation. An "A" can be appended to the instruction mnemonic for an Address register operation. An ".S" can be appended to force a short-form conditional branch instruction.

Mnemonic choices are summarized in Table A-1 under these headings:

Primary Mnemonic	Lists the nominal mnemonic form.
Alternate Mnemonic	Lists the alternate choices that can be used in place of the primary mnemonic.
Operand	Shows the operand category to which the primary and alternate mnemonics apply. xx is any allowed operand selection.
Description	Identifies the operation.

For simplicity, only the primary mnemonics are shown in the instruction set tables that follow.

Note that there are no mnemonic alternates for the instruction variations X (Extend), M (Multiple), and P (Peripheral Data). These suffixes cannot be omitted from their respective instruction mnemonics.

Bear in mind that the assembler will select the "Quick" version of an instruction (e.g., MOVEQ, ADDQ, SUBQ) whenever possible. Thus you can use the alternates for these mnemonics — the more general MOVE, ADD and SUB — without sacrificing any opportunities for code shortening.

For example: MOVE.L #40,D2
is coded as: MOVEQ #40,D2

Another example: ADD #1, D0
is coded as: ADDQ.W #1,D0

STATUS

The effect of instruction execution on the status bits is listed in Table A-2. The status bits are:

T — Trace mode
S — Supervisor state
X — Extend bit
N — Negative (or Sign) bit
Z — Zero bit
V — Overflow bit
C — Carry bit

The following symbols are used in the STATUS columns:

X — flag is affected by operation
(blank) — flag is not affected by operation
1 — flag is set by operation
0 — flag is cleared by operation

OPERATION PERFORMED

This column shows the sequence of operations that occurs when the instruction is executed. (Instruction fetches are not shown, nor is the incrementing of the Program Counter for the purpose of instruction fetches.) Each operation is generally shown in the following form:

destination   ←   source

indicating that the source contents move to the destination, replacing the destination contents. For example, the LEA instruction operation is:

[An]   ←   jadr

The effective address, which may be any of the jadr forms, is loaded into the specified Address register.

Following the arrow sequence is a description of the operation in words.

ABBREVIATIONS

Following are the abbreviations used for instruction formats and operation descriptions.

addr	Direct address (16 or 32 bits)
An	Address registers, n = 0-7 (8, 16, or 32 bits, depending on the instruction size)
bitb	Bit number of byte 0-7
bitl	Bit number of long word 0-31
cc	Condition code:

CC	Carry clear	0100
CS	Carry set	0101
EQ	Equal	0111
F	False	0001
GE	Greater than or equal	1100
GT	Greater than	1110
HI	High	0010
LE	Less than or equal	1111
LS	Low or same	0011
LT	Less than	1101
MI	Minus	1011
NE	Not equal	0110
PL	Plus	1010
T	True	0000
VC	No overflow	1000
VS	Overflow	1001

CCR	Condition Code register — the low-order byte of the Status register
count	Shift count (1-8)
dadr	Destination address, which may be any of the following addressing modes:

(An)	Register indirect
(An)+	Register indirect with postincrement
−(An)	Register indirect with predecrement
d16(An)	Register indirect with displacement
d8(An,i)	Register indirect, indexed
addr	Direct address

dAn	Destination Address register. This form is used only when there are two An operands.
aDn	Destination Data register. This form is used only when there are two Dn operands.
data3	3 bits of immediate data
data8	8 bits of immediate data
data16	16 bits of immediate data
data32	32 bits of immediate data

Dn   Data register, n = 0-7 (8, 16, or 32 bits, depending on instructio size)

d8   8-bit address displacement. Required, even if zero on indexe instructions.

d16   16-bit address displacement

i   Index register (An or Dn)

jadr   Jump address — same as sadr except no (An)+ or −(An)

label   Address label

madr   Multiple-instruction address — same as dadr except no (An)+ c −(An)

reg-list Register list naming one or more registers, each item in the li separated by a comma. Items may have the form:

Dn	Single data register
An	Single address register
rn_1-rn	Range of registers

rd   Destination registers (dDn or dAn)

rs   Source register (sDn or sAn)

sadr   Source address, which may be any of the following address mode

(An)	Register indirect
(An)+	Register indirect with postincrement
−(An)	Register indirect with predecrement
d16(An)	Register indirect with displacement
d8(An,i)	Register indirect, indexed
addr	Direct address
label	Program relative
label (i)	Program relative, indexed

sAn   Source Address register. This form is used only when there are tw An operands.

sDn   Source Data register. This form is used only when there are tw Dn operands.

SR   Status register (16 bits)

USP   User Stack Pointer. Note that this is Register A7.

vector   Trap address vector, the memory location containing the addres of the Trap routine.

[[ ]]   The contents of the memory location whose address is containe in the designated register (indirect memory addressing, or implied addressing).

[ ]   The contents of a register or memory location (register addressin or direct memory addressing).

For example:

$$[Dn] \leftarrow [[An]]$$

indicates that the contents of the memory location addressed by Register An are loaded into Dn, whereas:

$$[Dn] \leftarrow [An]$$

indicates that the contents of Register An itself are loaded into Dn

$\overline{x}$	Complement the value of x.
$x<y\text{-}z>$	Bits y through z of x. For example, $Dn<0\text{-}7>$ means the low-order byte of Dn. If the z term is omitted, then only the bit selected by y is being referenced. Thus $Dn<0>$ means the least significant bit of Dn.
+	Add
−	Subtract
x	Multiply
÷	Divide
$\wedge$	Logical AND
$\vee$	Logical OR
⊻	Logical Exclusive-OR
=	Equals
←	Data move in the direction of the arrow
←→	Data are exchanged between two locations

Table A-1. Alternate Instruction Mnemonics

Primary Mnemonic	Alternate Mnemonic	Operand	Description
ADD. B	ADDI. B	data8,xx	Add Immediate Byte
ADD. W	ADD	xx,xx	Add Word
	ADDA.W	xx,An	Add Address Register Word
	ADDI. W	data16,xx	Add Immediate Word
ADD. L	ADDA.L	xx,An	Add Address Register Long
	ADDI.L	data32,xx	Add Immediate Long
ADDQ.B	ADD.B	data3,xx	Add Quick Byte
ADDQ.W	ADD	data3,xx	Add Quick Word
	ADD. W		
ADDQ.L	ADD. L	data3,xx	Add Quick Long
AND.B	ANDI.B	data8,xx	AND Immediate Byte
AND.W	AND	xx,xx	AND Word
	ANDI.W	data16,xx	AND Immediate Word
AND. L	ANDI.L	data32,xx	AND Immediate Long
Bcc	Bcc.S	xx	Conditional Branch Short
CLR.W	CLR	xx	Clear Word
CMP.B	CMPI.B	data8,xx	Compare Immediate Byte
CMP.W	CMP	xx,xx	Compare Word
	CMPA.W	xx,An	Compare Address Register Word
	CMPI.W	data16,xx	Compare Immediate Word
CMP. L	CMPA.L	xx,An	Compare Address Register Long
	CMPI.L	data32,xx	Compare Immediate Long
EOR.B	EORI. B	data8,xx	Exclusive OR Immediate Byte
EOR. W	EOR	xx,xx	Exclusive OR Word
	EORI. W	data16,xx	Exclusive OR Immediate Word
EOR. L	EORI. L	data32,xx	Exclusive OR Immediate Long
MOVE. W	MOVE	xx,xx	Move Word
	MOVEA. W	xx,An	Move Address Register Word
MOVE. L	MOVEA.L	xx,An	Move Address Register Long
MOVEQ	MOVE. L	data8,xx	Move Quick (always Long)
OR. B	ORI. B	data8,xx	OR Immediate Byte
OR. W	OR	xx,xx	OR Word
	ORI. W	data16,xx	OR Immediate Word
OR. L	ORI. L	data32,xx	OR Immediate Long
SUB. B	SUBI. B	data8,xx	Subtract Immediate Byte
SUB.W	SUB.	xx,xx	Subtract Word
	SUBA. W	xx,An	Subtract Address Register Word
	SUBI.W	data16,xx	Subtract Immediate Word
SUB. L	SUBA. L	xx,An	Subtract Address Register Long
	SUBI. L	data32,xx	Subtract Immediate Long
SUBQ. B	SUB. B	data3,xx	Subtract Quick Byte
SUBQ. W	SUB	data3,xx	Subtract Quick Word
	SUB.W		
SUBQ.L	SUB. L	data3,xx	Subtract Quick Long

Table A-2. MC68000 Instruction Set Summary

Mnemonic	Operand(s)	Bytes	Clock Cycles	T	S	X	N	Z	V	C	Operation Performed
LEA	jadr,An	2,4, or 6	2(0/0)+								[An] — jadr Load effective address into specified address register. The addressing size is long, although the address loaded may be byte, word, or long, depending on how it is subsequently used.[2]
MOVE.B	(An),Dn	2	8(2/0)				×	×	0	0	[Dn<0-7>] — [[An]] Register indirect
	(An)+,Dn	2	8(2/0)				×	×	0	0	[Dn<0-7>] — [[An]], [An] — [An] + 1 Register indirect with postincrement[1]
	−(An),Dn	2	10(2/0)				×	×	0	0	[An] — [An] − 1, [Dn<0-7>] — [[An]] Register indirect with predecrement[1]
	d16(An),Dn	4	12(3/0)				×	×	0	0	[Dn<0-7>] — [[An] + d16] Register indirect with displacement
	d8(An,i),Dn	4	14(3/0)				×	×	0	0	[Dn<0-7>] — [[An] + d8 + [i]] Register indirect, indexed
	addr,Dn	4 or 6	4(1/0)+				×	×	0	0	[Dn<0-7>] — [[addr] Direct address
	label,Dn	4	12(3/0)				×	×	0	0	[Dn<0-7>] — [[PC] + d16] Program relative
	label(i),Dn	4	14(3/0)				×	×	0	0	[Dn<0-7>] — [[PC] + d8 + [i]] Program relative, indexed Load byte to data register from memory location specified by any of the addressing modes above. Bits 8-31 of the data register are not affected.
MOVE.B	Dn,(An)	2	9(1/1)				×	×	0	0	[[An]] — [Dn<0-7>] Register indirect
	Dn,(An)+	2	9(1/1)				×	×	0	0	[[An]] — [Dn<0-7>], [An] — [An] + 1 Register indirect with postincrement[1]
	Dn,−(An)	2	9(1/1)				×	×	0	0	[An] — [An] − 1, [[An]] — [Dn<0-7>] Register indirect with predecrement[1]
	Dn,d16(An)	4	13(2/1)				×	×	0	0	[[An] + d16] — [Dn<0-7>] Register indirect with displacement
	Dn,d8(An, i)	4	15(2/1)				×	×	0	0	[[An] + d8 + [i]] — [Dn<0-7>] Register indirect, indexed
	Dn,addr	4 or 6	5(0/1)+				×	×	0	0	[addr] — [Dn<0-7>] Direct address Store byte from data register to memory location specified by any of the addressing modes above.
MOVE.B	sadr,dadr	2,4 6, 8 or 10	5(1/1)+				×	×	0	0	[dadr] — [sadr] Store byte from specified source memory location to specified destination memory location.[1]

(Braces in the table group the register-to-memory operands as "sadr" and the memory-to-register operands as "dadr".)

I/O and Primary Memory Reference

Notes:

1. Postincrement and predecrement change by 1, unless the address register specified is the Stack Pointer (A7), where the address is changed by 2 rather than 1 to keep the Stack Pointer on a word boundary.
2. The effective address must be on an even word boundary (0000, 0002, 0004, etc.).
3. Postincrement and predecrement change by 2.
4. Postincrement and predecrement change by 4.

Table A-2. MC68000 Instruction Set Summary (Continued)

Mnemonic	Operand(s)	Bytes	Clock Cycles	T	S	X	N	Z	V	C	Operation Performed
MOVE.W	sadr, Dn	2, 4 or 6	4(1/0)+				×	×	0	0	$[Dn<0\text{-}15>] \leftarrow [sadr]$ — Load word to data register from memory location. Bits 16-31 of the data register are not affected.[2,3]
MOVE.W	sadr,An	2, 4 or 6	4(1/0)+								$[An]<0\text{-}15>] \leftarrow [sadr]$; $[An<16\text{-}31>] \leftarrow [An<15>]$ — Load word to address register from memory location. The sign is extended to all upper bits of the register.[2,3]
MOVE.W	rs,dadr	2, 4 or 6	5(0/1)+				×	×	0	0	$[dadr] \leftarrow [rs<0\text{-}15>]$ — Store word to memory location from data or address register.[2,3]
MOVE.W	sadr,dadr	2, 4 6, 8 or 10	5(0/1)+				×	×	0	0	$[dadr] \leftarrow [sadr]$ — Store word from source memory location to destination memory location.[2,3]
MOVE.L	sadr,Dn	2, 4 or 6	4(1/0)+				×	×	0	0	$[Dn<0\text{-}31>] \leftarrow [sadr]$ — Load long word to data register from memory location.[2,3]
MOVE.L	sadr,An	2, 4 or 6	8(2/0)+								$[An<0\text{-}31>] \leftarrow [sadr]$ — Load long word to address register from memory location.[2,4]
MOVE.L	rs,dadr	2, 4 or 6	10(0/2)+				×	×	0	0	$[dadr] \leftarrow [rs<0\text{-}31>]$ — Store long word from data or address register to memory location.[2,4]
MOVE.L	sadr,dadr	2, 4 6, 8 or 10	14(1/2)+				×	×	0	0	$[dadr] \leftarrow [sadr]$ — Store long word from source memory location to destination memory location.[2,4]
MOVEM.W	jadr,reg-list	4, 6 or 8	8 + 4n(2 + n/0)+								$[reg_1<0\text{-}15>] \leftarrow [[An]], [reg_1<16\text{-}31>] \leftarrow [reg_1<15>]$; $[reg_2<0\text{-}15>] \leftarrow [[An + 2]], [reg_2<16\text{-}31>] \leftarrow [reg_2<15>]$; $[reg_3<0\text{-}15>] \leftarrow [[An + 4]], [reg_3<16\text{-}31>] \leftarrow [reg_3<15>]$ . . . $[reg_n<0\text{-}15>] \leftarrow [[An + 2n\text{-}2]], [reg_n<16\text{-}31>] \leftarrow [reg_n<15>]$ — Load multiple words from sequential memory locations to specified registers, in order D0-D7, A0-A7. The sign is extended to all upper bits of the register.[2]
MOVEM.W	(An)+,reg-list	4	8 + 4n(2 + n/0)								$[reg_1<0\text{-}15>] \leftarrow [[An]], [reg_1<16\text{-}31>] \leftarrow [reg_1<15>], [An] \leftarrow [An + 2]$; $[reg_2<0\text{-}15>] \leftarrow [[An]], [reg_2<16\text{-}31>] \leftarrow [reg_2<15>], [An] \leftarrow [An + 2]$; $[reg_3<0\text{-}15>] \leftarrow [[An]], [reg_3<16\text{-}31>] \leftarrow [reg_3<15>], [An] \leftarrow [An + 2]$ . . . $[reg_n<0\text{-}15>] \leftarrow [[An]], [reg_n<16\text{-}31>] \leftarrow [reg_n<15>], [An] \leftarrow$ — Same as above except with postincrement.[3]

I/O and Primary Memory Reference (Continued)

Table A-2. MC68000 Instruction Set Summary (Continued)

Mnemonic	Operand(s)	Bytes	Clock Cycles	T	S	X	N	Z	V	C	Operation Performed
MOVEM.W	reg-list,madr	4, 6 or 8	4 + 5n(1/n)+								$[[An]] \leftarrow [reg1 <0\text{-}15>]$ $[An + 2]] \leftarrow [reg2 <0\text{-}15>]$ $[An + 4]] \leftarrow [reg3 <0\text{-}15>]$ . . . Store multiple words to sequential memory locations from specified registers, in order D0-D7, A0-A7.[2]
MOVEM.W	reg-list,−(An)	4	4 + 5n(1/n)+								$[[An + (2n\text{-}2)] \leftarrow [regn <0\text{-}15>]$ . . . $[An] \leftarrow [An\text{-}2].[[An]] \leftarrow [regn <0\text{-}15>]$ $[An] \leftarrow [An\text{-}2].[[An]] \leftarrow [reg2 <0\text{-}15>]$ $[An] \leftarrow [An\text{-}2].[[An]] \leftarrow [reg1 <0\text{-}15>]$ Store multiple words to sequential memory locations with predecrement to specified registers, in order A7-A0, D7-D0.[2, 3]
MOVEM.L	jadr,reg-list (An)+,reg-list reg-list,madr reg-list,−(An)	4, 6 or 8 / 4 / 4, 6 or 8 / 4	8 + 8n(2 + 2n/0) 8 + 8n(2 + 2n/0) 4 + 10n(1/n)+ 4 + 10n(1/n)								Same as MOVEM.W except that all 32 bits of the registers are moved.[2, 4]
MOVEP.W	d16(An),Dn	4	16(4/0)								$[Dn <8\text{-}15>] \leftarrow [[An] + d16].[An] \leftarrow [An] + 2$ $[Dn <0\text{-}7>] \leftarrow [[An] + d16]$ Load peripheral data bytes from alternate memory locations to data register word. The address is a byte address.[3]
MOVEP.W	Dn,d16(An)	4	18(2/2)								$[[An] + d16] \leftarrow [Dn <8\text{-}15>].[An] \leftarrow [An] + 2$ $[[An] + d16] \leftarrow [Dn <0\text{-}7>]$ Store peripheral data bytes from data register long to alternate memory locations. The address is a byte address.[3]
MOVEP.L	dos(An),Dn	4	24(6/0)								$[Dn <24\text{-}31>] \leftarrow [[An] + d16].[An] \leftarrow [An] + 2$ $[Dn <16\text{-}23>] \leftarrow [[An] + d16].[An] \leftarrow [An] + 2$ $[Dn <8\text{-}15>] \leftarrow [[An] + d16].[An] \leftarrow [An] + 2$ $[Dn <0\text{-}7>] \leftarrow [[An] + d16]$ Load peripheral data bytes from alternate memory locations to data register long. The address is a byte address.[3]
MOVEP.L	Dn,d16(An)	4	28(2/4)								$[[An] + d16] \leftarrow [Dn <24\text{-}31>].[An] \leftarrow [An] + 2$ $[[An] + d16] \leftarrow [Dn <16\text{-}23>].[An] \leftarrow [An] + 2$ $[[An] + d16] \leftarrow [Dn <8\text{-}15>].[An] \leftarrow [An] + 2$ $[[An] + d16] \leftarrow [Dn <0\text{-}7>]$ Store peripheral data bytes from data register long to alternate memory locations. The address is a byte address.[3]

I/O and Primary Memory Reference (Continued)

Table A-2. MC68000 Instruction Set Summary (Continued)

Secondary Memory Reference (Memory Operate)

Mnemonic	Operand(s)	Bytes	Clock Cycles	T	S	X	N	Z	V	C	Operation Performed
ABCD	-(sAn),-(dAn)	2	19(3/1)			X	U	U	U	X	[sAn] ← [sAn] - 1; [dAn] ← [dAn]-1; [[dAn]] ← [[dAn]] + [[sAn]] + X; Add decimal memory byte to memory byte with carry (Extend bit). Both addresses are byte.[1]
ADD.B	sadr,Dn	2, 4 or 6	4(1/0)+			X	X	X	X	X	[Dn<0-7>] ← [Dn<0-7>] + [sadr]; Add byte to data register from memory location. Bits 8-31 of the data register are not affected.[1]
ADD.B	Dn,dadr	2, 4 or 6	9(1/1)+			X	X	X	X	X	[dadr] ← [dadr] + [Dn<0-7>]; Add byte to memory location from data register.[1]
ADD.W	sadr,Dn	2, 4 or 6	4(1/0)+			X	X	X	X	X	[Dn<0-15>] ← [Dn<0-15>] + [sadr]; Add word to data register from memory location. Bits 16-31 of the data register are not affected.[2,3]
ADD.W	sadr,An	2, 4 or 6	8(1/0)+								[An<0-31>] ← [An<0-31>] + [sadr] (sign extended); Add word to address register from memory location. The sign of the memory word is extended to a full 32 bits for the operation.[2,3]
ADD.W	Dn,Dadr	2, 4 or 6	9(1/1)+			X	X	X	X	X	[dadr] ← [dadr] + [Dn<0-15>]; Add word to memory location from data register.[2,3]
ADD.L	sadr,Dn	2, 4 or 6	6(1/0)+			X	X	X	X	X	[Dn<0-31>] ← [Dn<0-31>] + [sadr]; Add long word to data registers from memory location.[2,4]
ADD.L	sadr,An	2, 4 or 6	6(1/0)+								[An<0-31>] ← [An<0-31>] + [sadr]; Add long word to address register from memory location.[2,4]
ADD.L	Dn,dadr	2, 4 or 6	14(1/2)+			X	X	X	X	X	[dadr] ← [dadr] + [Dn<0-31>]; Add long word to memory locations from data register.[2,4]
ADDX.B	-(sAn),-(dAn)	2	19(3/1)			X	X	X	X	X	[sAn] ← [sAn] - 1; [dAn] ← [dAn] - 1; [[dAn]] ← [[dAn]] + [[sAn]] + X; Add memory byte to memory byte with carry (Extend bit). Both addresses are byte.[1]
ADDX.W	-(sAn),-(dAn)	2	19(3/1)			X	X	X	X	X	[sAn] ← [sAn] - 2; [dAn] ← [dAn] - 2; [[dAn]] ← [[dAn]] + [[sAn]] + X; Add memory word to memory word with carry (Extend bit). Both address are word.[2,3]
ADDX.L	-(sAn),-(dAn)	2	32(5/2)			X	X	X	X	X	[sAn] ← [sAn] - 4; [dAn] ← [dAn] - 4; [[dAn]] ← [[dAn]] + [[sAn]] + X; Add memory long word to memory long word with carry (Extend bit). Both addresses are long word.[2,4]
AND.B	sadr,Dn	2, 4 or 6	4(1/0)+				X	X	0	0	[Dn<0-7>] ← [Dn<0-7>] ∧ [sadr]; AND byte to data register from memory location. Bits 8-31 of the data register are not affected.[1]
AND.B	Dn,dadr	2, 4 or 6	9(1/1)+				X	X	0	0	[dadr] ← [dadr] ∧ [Dn<0-7>]; AND byte to memory location from data register.[1]

Table A-2. MC68000 Instruction Set Summary (Continued)

Mnemonic	Operand(s)	Bytes	Clock Cycles	T	S	X	N	Z	V	C	Operation Performed
AND.W	sadr,Dn	2, 4 or 6	4(1/0)+				x	x	0	0	[Dn<0-15>] — [Dn<0-15>] ∧ [sadr] AND word to data register from memory location. Bits 16-31 of the data register are not affected.[2, 3]
AND.W	Dn,dadr	2, 4 or 6	9(1/1)+				x	x	0	0	[dadr] — [dadr] ∧ [Dn<0-15>] AND word to memory location from data register.[2, 3]
AND.L	sadr,Dn	2, 4 or 6	6(1/0)+				x	x	0	0	[Dn<0-31>] — [Dn<0-31>] ∧ [sadr] AND long word to data register from memory location.[2, 4]
AND.L	Dn,dadr	2, 4 or 6	14(1/2)+				x	x	0	0	[dadr] — [dadr] ∧ [Dn<0-31>] AND long word to memory location from data register.[2, 4]
CLR.B	dadr	2, 4 or 6	9(1/1)+				0	1	0	0	[dadr] — 0 Clear memory byte to zeroes.[1]
CLR.W	dadr	2, 4 or 6	9(1/1)+				0	1	0	0	[dadr] — 0 Clear memory word to zeroes. 2, 3
CLR.L	dadr	2, 4 or 6	14(1/2)+				0	1	0	0	[dadr] — 0 Clear memory long word to zeroes.[2, 4]
CMP.B	sadr,Dn	2, 4 or 6	4(1/0)+				x	x	x	x	[Dn<0-7>] – [sadr] Compare data register byte with memory byte and set condition codes accordingly. Register/memory data are not changed on any compares.[1]
CMP.W	sadr,Dn	2, 4 or 6	4(1/0)+				x	x	x	x	[Dn<0-15>] – [sadr] Compare data register word with memory word and set condition codes accordingly.[2, 3]
CMP.W	sadr,An	2, 4 or 6	6(1/0)+				x	x	x	x	[An<0-15>] – [sadr] Compare address register word with memory word and set condition codes accordingly.[2, 3]
CMP.L	sadr,Dn	2, 4 or 6	6(1/0)+				x	x	x	x	[Dn<0-31>] – [sadr] Compare data register with memory long word and set condition codes accordingly.[2, 4]
CMP.L	sadr,An	2, 4 or 6	6(1/0)+				x	x	x	x	[An<0-31>] – [sadr] Compare address register with memory long word and set condition codes accordingly.[2, 4]
CMPM.B	(sAn)+,(dAn)+	2	12(3/0)				x	x	x	x	[[dAn]] – [[sAn]] [dAn] — [dAn] + 1 [sAn] — [sAn] + 1 Compare memory bytes and set condition codes accordingly. The memory data are not changed on any compares.[1]
CMPM.W	(sAn)+,(dAn)+	2	12(3/0)				x	x	x	x	[[dAn]] – [[sAn]] [dAn] — [dAn] + 2 [sAn] — [sAn] + 2 Compare memory words and set condition codes accordingly.[2, 3]
CMPM.L	(sAn)+,(dAn)+	2	20(5/0)				x	x	x	x	[[dAn]] – [[sAn]] [dAn] — [dAn] + 4 [sAn] — [sAn] + 4 Compare memory long words and set condition codes accordingly.[2, 4]

Secondary Memory Reference (Memory Operate) (Continued)

Table A-2. MC68000 Instruction Set Summary (Continued)

Mnemonic	Operand(s)	Bytes	Clock Cycles	Status							Operation Performed
				T	S	X	N	Z	V	C	
DIVS	sadr,Dn	2, 4 or 6	<158(1/0)+				X	X	X	0	[Dn<0-15>] — [Dn<0-31>] ÷ [sadr] / [Dn<16-31>] — remainder / Divide signed numbers. Division by zero causes a TRAP. The source address is a word address.[2, 3]
DIVU	sadr,Dn	2, 4 or 6	≤140(1/0)+				X	X	X	0	[Dn<0-15>] — [Dn<0-31>] ÷ [sadr] / [Dn<16-31>] — remainder / Divide unsigned numbers. Division by zero causes a TRAP. The source address is a word address.[2, 3]
EORB	Dn,dadr	2, 4 or 6	9(1/1)+				X	X	0	0	[dadr] — [dadr] ↤ [Dn<0-7>] / Exclusive-OR byte to memory location from data register.[1]
EORW	Dn,dadr	2, 4 or 6	9(1/1)+				X	X	0	0	[dadr] — [dadr] ↤ [Dn<0-15>] / Exclusive-OR word to memory location from data registers.[2, 3]
EORL	Dn,dadr	2, 4 or 6	14(1/2)+				X	X	0	0	[dadr] — [dadr] ↤ [Dn<0-31>] / Exclusive-OR long word to memory location from data register.[2, 4]
MULS	sadr,Dn	2, 4 or 6	<70(1/0)+				X	X	0	0	[Dn<0-31>] — [Dn<0-15>] × [sadr] / Multiply two 16-bit signed numbers, yielding a 32-bit signed product. The source address is a word address.[2, 3]
MULU	sadr,Dn	2, 4 or 6	<74(2/0)+				X	X	0	0	[Dn<0-31>] — [Dn<0-15>] × [sadr] / Multiply two 16-bit unsigned numbers, yielding a 32-bit unsigned product. The source address is a word address.[2, 3]
NBCD	dadr	2, 4 or 6	9(1/1)+			X	U	U	U	X	[dadr] — 0 — [dadr] — X / Negate decimal memory byte. This operation produces the tens complement if X = 0 or the nines complement if X = 1.
NEGB	dadr	2, 4 or 6	9(1/1)+			X	X	X	X	X	[dadr] — 0 — [dadr] / Negate memory byte.[1]
NEGW	dadr	2, 4 or 6	9(1/1)+			X	X	X	X	X	[dadr] — 0 — [dadr] / Negate memory word.[2, 3]
NEGL	dadr	2, 4 or 6	14(1/2)+			X	X	X	X	X	[dadr] — 0 — [dadr] / Negate memory long word.[2, 4]
NEGX.B	dadr	2, 4 or 6	9(1/1)+			X	X	X	X	X	[dadr] — 0 — [dadr] — X / Negate memory byte with Extend bit.[1]
NEGX.W	dadr	2, 4 or 6	9(1/1)+			X	X	X	X	X	[dadr] — 0 — [dadr] — X / Negate memory word with Extend bit.[2, 3]
NEGXL	dadr	2, 4 or 6	14(1/2)+			X	X	X	X	X	[dadr] — 0 — [dadr] — X / Negate memory long word with Extend bit.[2, 4]
NOTB	dadr	2, 4 or 6	9(1/1)+				X	X	0	0	[dadr] — [dadr] / Ones complement memory byte.[1]
NOTW	dadr	2, 4 or 6	9(1/1)+				X	X	0	0	[dadr] — [dadr] / Ones complement memory word.[2, 3]
NOTL	dadr	2, 4 or 6	14(1/2)+				X	X	0	0	[dadr] — [dadr] / Ones complement memory long word.[2, 4]
ORB	sadr,Dn	2, 4 or 6	4(1/0)+				X	X	0	0	[Dn<0-7>] — [Dn<0-7>] ∨ [sadr] / OR byte to data register from memory location. Bits 8-31 of the data register are not affected.[1]
ORB	Dn,dadr	2, 4 or 6	9(1/1)+				X	X	0	0	[dadr] — [dadr] ∨ [Dn<0-7>] / OR byte to memory location from data register.[1]

Secondary Memory Reference (Memory Operate) (Continued)

Table A-2. MC68000 Instruction Set Summary (Continued)

Mnemonic	Operand(s)	Bytes	Clock Cycles	T	S	X	N	Z	V	C	Operation Performed
OR.W	sadr,Dn	2, 4 or 6	4(1/0)+				X	X	0	0	[Dn<0-15>] ← [Dn<0-15>] ∨ [sadr] OR word to data register from memory location. Bits 16-31 of the data register are not affected.[2, 3]
OR.W	Dn,dadr	2, 4 or 6	9(1/1)+				X	X	0	0	[dadr] ← [dadr] ∨ [Dn<0-15>] OR word to memory location from data register.[2, 3]
OR.L	sadr,Dn	2, 4 or 6	6(1/0)+				X	X	0	0	[Dn<0-31>] ← [Dn<0-31>] ∨ [sadr] OR long word to data register from memory location.[2, 4]
OR.L	Dn,dadr	2, 4 or 6	14(1/2)+				X	X	0	0	[dadr] ← [dadr] ∨ [Dn<0-31>] OR long word to memory location from data register.[2, 4]
SBCD	-(sAn),-(dAn)	2	19(3/1)			X	U	U	U	X	[sAn] ← [sAn] - 1 [dAn] ← [dAn] - 1 [[dAn]] ← [[dAn]] - [[sAn]] - X Subtract decimal memory byte from memory byte with carry (Extend bit). Both addresses are byte.[1]
SCC	dadr	2, 4 or 6	9(1/1)+								[dadr] ← [all 1's if cc = TRUE [dadr] ← [all 0's if cc = FALSE Set status in memory byte.[1]
SUB.B	sadr,Dn	2, 4 or 6	4(1/0)+			X	X	X	X	X	[Dn<0-7>] ← [Dn<0-7>] - [sadr] Subtract memory byte from byte in data register. Bits 8-31 of the data register are not affected.[1]
SUB.B	Dn,dadr	2, 4 or 6	9(1/1)+			X	X	X	X	X	[dadr] ← [dadr] - [Dn<0-7>] Subtract byte in data register from memory byte.[1]
SUB.W	sadr,Dn	2, 4 or 6	4(1/0)+			X	X	X	X	X	[Dn<0-15>] ← [Dn<0-15>] - [sadr] Subtract memory word from word in data register. Bits 16-31 of the data register are not affected.[2, 3]
SUB.W	sadr,An	2, 4 or 6	8(1/0)+			X	X	X	X	X	[An<0-31>] ← [An<0-31>] - [sadr] (sign extended) Subtract memory word from address register contents. The sign of the memory word is extended to a full 32 bits for the operation.[2, 3]
SUB.W	Dn,dadr	2, 4 or 6	9(1/1)+			X	X	X	X	X	[dadr] ← [dadr] - [Dn<0-15>] Subtract data register word from memory location word.[2, 3]
SUB.L	sadr,Dn	2, 4 or 6	6(1/0)+			X	X	X	X	X	[Dn<0-31>] ← [Dn<0-31>] - [sadr] Subtract memory long word from data register contents.[2, 4]
SUB.L	sadr,An	2, 4 or 6	6(1/0)+			X	X	X	X	X	[An<0-31>] ← [An<0-31>] - [sadr] Subtract memory long word from address register contents.[2, 4]
SUB.L	Dn,dadr	2, 4 or 6	14(1/2)+			X	X	X	X	X	[dadr] ← [dadr] - [Dn<0-31>] Subtract contents of data register from memory long word.[2, 4]
SUBX.B	-(sAn),-(dAn)	2	19(3/1)			X	X	X	X	X	[sAn] ← [sAn] - 1 [dAn] ← [dAn] - 1 [[dAn]] ← [[dAn]] - [[sAn]] - X Subtract memory byte from memory byte with borrow (Extend bit). Both addresses are byte.[1]
SUBX.W	-(sAn),-(dAn)	2	19(3/1)			X	X	X	X	X	[sAn] ← [sAn] - 2 [dAn] ← [dAn] - 2 [[dAn]] ← [[dAn]] - [[sAn]] - X Subtract memory word from memory word with borrow (Extend bit). Both addresses are word.[2, 3]

Secondary Memory Reference (Memory Operate) (Continued)

Table A-2. MC68000 Instruction Set Summary (Continued)

Category	Mnemonic	Operand(s)	Bytes	Clock Cycles	T	S	X	N	Z	V	C	Operation Performed
I/O and Primary Memory Reference (Continued)	SUBX.L	–(sAn),–(dAn)	2	32(5/2)			X	X	X	X	X	[sAn] ← [sAn] – 4 [dAn] ← [dAn] – 4 [[dAn]] ← [[dAn]] – [[sAn]] – X Subtract memory long word from memory long word with borrow (Extend bit). Both addresses are long word.[2,4]
	TAS	dadr	2, 4 or 6	11(1/1)+				X	X	0	0	[dadr<7>] ← 1 Test status of memory byte and set high-order bit to 1.
	TST.B	dadr	2, 4 or 6	4(1/0)+				X	X	0	0	[dadr] ← 0 Test status of memory byte. The byte value is not changed.
	TST.W	dadr	2, 4 or 6	4(1/0)+				X	X	0	0	[dadr] ← 0 Test status of memory word. The word value is not changed.
	TST.L	dadr	2, 4 or 6	4(1/0)+				X	X	0	0	[dadr] ← 0 Test status of memory long word. The long word value is not changed.
Immediate	MOVEQ	data8,Dn	2	4(1/0)				X	X	0	0	[Dn<0-7>] ← data8 [Dn<8-32>] ← [Dn<7>] Load immediate data byte to data register. The sign is extended to all upper bits of the data register.
	MOVE.B	data8,Dn	4	8(2/0)				X	X	0	0	[Dn<0-7>] ← data8 Load immediate data byte to data register. Bits 8-31 of the data register are not affected.
	MOVE.B	data8,dadr	4, 6 or 8	9(1/1)+				X	X	0	0	[dadr] ← [data8] Load immediate data byte into memory location.[1]
	MOVE.W	data16,Dn	4	8(2/0)				X	X	0	0	[Dn<0-15>] ← data16 Load immediate data word to data register. Bits 16-31 of the data register are not affected.
	MOVE.W	data16,An	4	8(2/0)								[An<0-15>] ← data16 [An<16-31>] ← [An<15>] Load immediate data word to address register. The sign is extended to all upper bits of the register.
	MOVE.W	data16,dadr	4, 6 or 8	9(1/1)+				X	X	0	0	[dadr] ← data16 Load immediate data word into memory location.[2,3]
	MOVE.L	data32,Dn	6	12(3/0)				X	X	0	0	[Dn<0-31>] ← data32 Load immediate data long word into data register.
	MOVE.L	data32,An	6	12(3/0)								[An<0-31>] ← data32 Load immediate data long word into address register.
	MOVE.L	data32,dadr	6, 8 or 10	18(2/2)+				X	X	0	0	[dadr] ← data32 Load immediate data long word into memory location.[2,4]
Immediate Operate	ADD.B	data8,Dn	4	8(2/0)			X	X	X	X	X	[Dn<0-7>] ← [Dn<0-7>] + data8 Add immediate data byte to data register. Bits 8-31 of the data register are not affected.
	ADD.B	data8,dadr	4, 6 or 8	13(2/1)+			X	X	X	X	X	[dadr] ← [dadr] + data8 Add immediate data byte to memory location.[1]
	ADD.W	data16,Dn	4	8(2/0)			X	X	X	X	X	[Dn<0-15>] ← [Dn<0-15>] + data16 Add immediate data word to data register. Bits 16-31 of the data register are not affected.

Table A-2. MC68000 Instruction Set Summary (Continued)

Mnemonic	Operand(s)	Bytes	Clock Cycles	T	S	X	N	Z	V	C	Operation Performed
ADD.W	data16,An	4	8(2/0)								$[An<0\text{-}31>] \leftarrow [An<0\text{-}31>] + \text{data } 16$ (sign extended) Add immediate data word to address register. The sign of the data word is extended to a full 32 bits for the operation.
ADD.W	data16,dadr	4, 6 or 8	13(2/1)+			×	×	×	×	×	$[\text{dadr}] \leftarrow [\text{dadr}] + \text{data16}$ Add immediate data word to memory location.[2, 3]
ADD.L	data32,Dn	6	16(3/0)			×	×	×	×	×	$[Dn<0\text{-}31>] \leftarrow [Dn<0\text{-}31>] + \text{data32}$ Add immediate data long word to data register.
ADD.L	data32,An	6	16(3/0)								$[An<0\text{-}31>] \leftarrow [An<0\text{-}31>] + \text{data32}$ Add immediate data long word to address register.
ADD.L	data32,dadr	6, 8 or 10	22(3/2)+			×	×	×	×	×	$[\text{dadr}] \leftarrow [\text{dadr}] + \text{data32}$ Add immediate data long word to memory location.[2, 4]
ADDQ.B	data3,Dn	2	4(1/0)			×	×	×	×	×	$[Dn<0\text{-}7>] \leftarrow [Dn<0\text{-}7>] + \text{data3}$ Add immediate three bits to data register byte. Bits 8-31 of the data register are not affected.
ADDQ.B	data3,dadr	2, 4 or 6	9(1/0)+			×	×	×	×	×	$[\text{dadr}] \leftarrow [\text{dadr}] + \text{data3}$ Add immediate three bits to memory byte.[1]
ADDQ.W	data3,Dn	2	4(1/0)			×	×	×	×	×	$[Dn<0\text{-}15>] \leftarrow [Dn<0\text{-}15>] + \text{data3}$ Add immediate three bits to data register word. Bits 16-31 of the data register are not affected.
ADDQ.W	data3,An	2	4(1/0)								$[An<0\text{-}15>] \leftarrow [An<0\text{-}15>] + \text{data3}$ Add immediate three bits to address register word. Bits 16-31 of the address register are not affected.
ADDQ.W	data3,dadr	2, 4 or 6	9(1/1)+			×	×	×	×	×	$[\text{dadr}] \leftarrow [\text{dadr}] + \text{data3}$ Add immediate three bits to memory word.[2, 3]
ADDQ.L	data3,Dn	2	8(1/0)			×	×	×	×	×	$[Dn<0\text{-}31>] \leftarrow [Dn<0\text{-}31>] + \text{data3}$ Add immediate three bits to data register long word.
ADDQ.L	data3,An	2	8(1/0)								$[An<0\text{-}31>] \leftarrow [An<0\text{-}31>] + \text{data3}$ Add immediate three bits to address register long word.
ADDQ.L	data3,dadr	2, 4 or 6	14(1/2)			×	×	×	×	×	$[\text{dadr}] \leftarrow [\text{dadr}] + \text{data3}$ Add immediate three bits to memory long word.[2, 4]
AND.B	data8,Dn	4	8(2/0)				×	×	0	0	$[Dn<0\text{-}7>] \leftarrow [Dn<0\text{-}7>] \wedge \text{data8}$ AND immediate data byte to data register. Bits 8-31 of the data register are not affected.
AND.B	data8,dadr	4, 6 or 8	13(2/1)+				×	×	0	0	$[\text{dadr}] \leftarrow [\text{dadr}] \wedge \text{data8}$ AND immediate data byte to memory byte.[1]
AND.W	data16,Dn	4	8(2/0)				×	×	0	0	$[Dn<0\text{-}15>] \leftarrow [Dn<0\text{-}15>] \wedge \text{data16}$ AND immediate data word to data register. Bits 16-31 of the data register are not affected.
AND.W	data16,dadr	4, 6 or 8	13(2/1)				×	×	0	0	$[\text{dadr}] \leftarrow [\text{dadr}] \wedge \text{data16}$ AND immediate data word to memory word.[2, 3]
AND.L	data32,Dn	6	16(3/0)				×	×	0	0	$[Dn<0\text{-}31>] \leftarrow [Dn<0\text{-}31>] \wedge \text{data32}$ AND immediate data long word to data register.
AND.L	data32,dadr	6, 8 or 10	22(3/2)+				×	×	0	0	$[\text{dadr}] \leftarrow [\text{dadr}] \wedge \text{data32}$ AND immediate data long word to memory.[2, 4]

Immediate Operate (Continued)

Table A-2. MC68000 Instruction Set Summary (Continued)

Mnemonic	Operand(s)	Bytes	Clock Cycles	T	S	X	N	Z	V	C	Operation Performed
CMP.B	data8,Dn	4	8(2/0)				X	X	X	X	[Dn<0-7>] − data8. Compare data register byte with immediate data byte and set condition codes accordingly. Register data are not changed on any compares.
CMP.B	data8,dadr	4, 6 or 8	8(2/0)+				X	X	X	X	[dadr] − data8. Compare memory byte with immediate data byte and set condition codes accordingly.[1]
CMP.W	data16,Dn	4	8(2/0)				X	X	X	X	[Dn<0-15>] − data16. Compare data register word with immediate data word and set condition codes accordingly.
CMP.W	data16,An	4	8(2/0)				X	X	X	X	[An<0-15>] − data 16. Compare address register word with immediate data word and set condition codes accordingly.
CMP.W	data16,dadr	4, 6 or 8	8(2/0)+				X	X	X	X	[dadr] − data16. Compare memory word with immediate data word and set condition codes accordingly.[2, 3]
CMP.L	data32,Dn	6	14(3/0)				X	X	X	X	[Dn<0-31>] − data32. Compare data register with immediate data long word and set condition codes accordingly.
CMP.L	data32,An	6	14(3/0)				X	X	X	X	[An<0-31>] − data32. Compare address register with immediate data long word and set condition codes accordingly.
CMP.L	data32,dadr	6, 8 or 10	12(3/0)+				X	X	X	X	[dadr] − data32. Compare memory long word with immediate data long word and set condition codes accordingly.[2, 4]
DIVS	data16,Dn	4	≤162(2/0)				X	X	X	0	[Dn<0-15>] − [Dn<0-31>] ÷ data16. [Dn<16-31>] − remainder. Divide signed numbers. Division by zero causes a TRAP.
DIVU	data16,Dn	4	≤148(2/0)				X	X	X	0	[Dn<0-15>] − [Dn<0-31>] ÷ data16. [Dn<16-31>] − remainder. Divide unsigned numbers. Division by zero causes a TRAP.
EOR.B	data8,Dn	4	8(2/0)				X	X	0	0	[Dn<0-7>] − [Dn<0-7>] ⊻ data8. Exclusive-OR data byte to data register. Bits 8-31 of the data register are not affected.
EOR.B	data8,dadr	4, 6 or 8	13(2/1)+				X	X	0	0	[dadr] − [dadr] ⊻ data8. Exclusive-OR data byte to memory byte.[1]
EOR.W	data16,Dn	4	8(2/0)				X	X	0	0	[Dn<0-15>] − [Dn<0-15>] ⊻ data16. Exclusive-OR data word to data register. Bits 16-31 of the data register are not affected.
EOR.W	data16,dadr	4, 6 or 8	13(2/1)+				X	X	0	0	[dadr] − [dadr] ⊻ data16. Exclusive-OR immediate data word to memory word.[2, 3]
EOR.L	data32,Dn	6	16(3/0)				X	X	0	0	[Dn<0-31>] − [Dn>0-31>] ⊻ data32. Exclusive-OR immediate data long word to data register.
EOR.L	data32,dadr	6, 8 or 10	22(3/2)+				X	X	0	0	[dadr] − [dadr] ⊻ data32. Exclusive-OR immediate data long word to memory.[2, 4]

Immediate Operate (Continued)

Table A-2. MC68000 Instruction Set Summary (Continued)

Immediate Operate (Continued)

Mnemonic	Operand(s)	Bytes	Clock Cycles	T	S	X	N	Z	V	C	Operation Performed
MULS	data16,Dn	4	≤74(2/0)				×	×	0	0	$[Dn<0\text{-}311>] \leftarrow [Dn<0\text{-}15>] \times data16$ — Multiply two 16-bit signed numbers, yielding a 32-bit signed product.
MULU	data16,Dn	4	≤74(2/0)				×	×	0	0	$[Dn<0\text{-}31>] \leftarrow [Dn<0\text{-}15>] \times data16$ — Multiply two 16-bit unsigned numbers, yielding a 32-bit unsigned product.
ORB	data8,Dn	4	8(2/0)				×	×	0	0	$[Dn<0\text{-}7>] \leftarrow [Dn<0\text{-}7>] \vee data8$ — OR immediate data byte to data register. Bits 8-31 of the data register are not affected.
ORB	data8,dadr	4, 6 or 8	13(2/1)+				×	×	0	0	$[dadr] \leftarrow [dadr] \vee data8$ — OR immediate data byte to memory byte.[1]
ORW	data16,Dn	4	8(2/0)				×	×	0	0	$[Dn<0\text{-}15>] \leftarrow [Dn<0\text{-}15>] \vee data16$ — OR immediate data word to data register. Bits 16-31 of the data register are not affected.
ORW	data16,dadr	4, 6 or 8	13(2/1)+				×	×	0	0	$[dadr] \leftarrow [dadr] \vee data16$ — OR immediate data word to memory word.[2,3]
ORL	data32,Dn	6	16(3/0)				×	×	0	0	$[Dn<0\text{-}31>] \leftarrow [Dn<0\text{-}31>] \vee data32$ — OR immediate data long word to data register.
ORL	data32,dadr	6, 8 or 10	22(3/2)+				×	×	0	0	$[dadr] \leftarrow [dadr] \vee data32$ — OR immediate data long word to memory.[2,4]
SUBB	data8,Dn	4	8(2/0)			×	×	×	×	×	$[Dn<0\text{-}7>] \leftarrow [Dn<0\text{-}7>] - data8$ — Subtract immediate data byte from data register. Bits 8-31 of the data register are not affected.
SUBB	data8,dadr	4, 6 or 8	13(2/1)+			×	×	×	×	×	$[dadr] \leftarrow [dadr] - data8$ — Subtract immediate data byte from memory byte.[1]
SUBW	data16,Dn	4	8(2/0)			×	×	×	×	×	$[Dn<0\text{-}15>] \leftarrow [Dn<0\text{-}15>] - data16$ — Subtract immediate data word from data register. Bits 16-31 of the data register are not affected.
SUBW	data16,An	4	8(2/0)								$[An<0\text{-}31>] \leftarrow [An<0\text{-}31>] - data16$ (sign extended) — Subtract immediate data word from address register. The sign of the data word is extended to a full 32 bits for the operation.
SUBW	data16,dadr	4, 6 or 8	13(2/1)+			×	×	×	×	×	$[dadr] \leftarrow [dadr] - data16$ — Subtract immediate data word from memory word.[2,3]
SUBL	data32,Dn	6	16(3/0)			×	×	×	×	×	$[Dn<0\text{-}31>] \leftarrow [Dn<0\text{-}31>] - data32$ — Subtract immediate long word from data register contents.
SUBL	data32,An	6	16(3/0)								$[An<0\text{-}31>] \leftarrow [An<0\text{-}31>] - data32$ — Subtract immediate data long word from address register.
SUBL	data32,dadr	6, 8 or 10	22(3/2)+			×	×	×	×	×	$[dadr] \leftarrow [dadr] - data32$ — Subtract immediate data long word from memory word.[2,4]
SUBQB	data3,Dn	2	4(1/0)			×	×	×	×	×	$[Dn<0\text{-}7>] \leftarrow [Dn<0\text{-}7>] - data3$ — Subtract immediate three bits from data register byte. Bits 8-31 of the data register are not affected.
SUBQB	data3,dadr	2, 4 or 6	9(1/1)+			×	×	×	×	×	$[dadr] \leftarrow [dadr] - data3$ — Subtract immediate three bits from memory byte.[1]

Table A-2. MC68000 Instruction Set Summary (Continued)

	Mnemonic	Operand(s)	Bytes	Clock Cycles	Status T	Status S	Status X	Status N	Status Z	Status V	Status C	Operation Performed
Immediate Operate (Continued)	SUBQ.W	data3,Dn	2	4(1/0)			X	X	X	X	X	[Dn <0-15>] ← [Dn <0>] – data3 Subtract immediate three bits from data register word. Bits 16-31 of the data register are not affected.
	SUBQ.W	data3,An	2	4(1/0)								[An <0-15>] ← [An <0-15>] – data3 Subtract immediate three bits from address register word. Bits 16-31 of the address register are not affected.
	SUBQ.W	data3,dadr	2, 4 or 6	9(1/1)+			X	X	X	X	X	[dadr] ← [dadr] – data3 Subtract immediate three bits from memory word.[2, 3]
	SUBQ.L	data3,Dn	2	8(1/0)			X	X	X	X	X	[Dn <0-31>] ← [Dn <0-31>] – data3 Subtract immediate three bits from data register contents.
	SUBQ.L	data3,An	2	8(1/0)								[An <0-31>] ← [An <0-31>] – data3 Subtract immediate three bits from address register contents.
	SUBQ.L	data3,dadr	2, 4 or 6	14(1/2)+			X	X	X	X	X	[dadr] ← [dadr] – data3 Subtract immediate three bits from memory long word.[2, 4]
JUMP, BRANCH	BRA	label	2 or 4	10(2/0)								[PC] ← label Branch unconditionally (short).
	JMP	jadr	2, 4 or 6	4(1/0)+								[PC] ← jadr Jump unconditionally.
Subroutine CALL and RETURN	BSR	label	2 or 4	10, 8(1/0) 10, 12(2/0)								[A7] ← [A7] – 2 [[A7]] ← [PC] [PC] ← label Branch to subroutine (short).
	JSR	jadr	2, 4 or 6	14(1/2)+								[A7] ← [A7] – 2 [[A7]] ← [PC] [PC] ← jadr Jump to subroutine.
	RTS		2	16(4/0)								[PC] ← [[A7]] [A7] ← [A7] + 2 Return from subroutine
	RTR		2	20(5/0)								[SR<0-4>] ← [[A7<0-4>]] [A7] ← [A7] + 2 [PC] ← [[A7]] [A7] ← [A7] + 2 Restore condition codes and return from subroutine.
Branch on Condition	Bcc	label	2 or 4	10, 8(1/0) 10, 12(2/0)								[PC] ← label Branch if condition met.
	DBcc	Dn,label	4	12(2/0) 10(2/0), 14(3/0)								If cc then no further action. [Dn <0-15>] ← [Dn <0-15>] – 1 If [Dn <0-15>] = –1 then no further action. [PC] ← label Test condition, decrement and branch. Loop until the specified condition is true or until the loop count is exhausted.

Table A-2. MC68000 Instruction Set Summary (Continued)

	Mnemonic	Operand(s)	Bytes	Clock Cycles	T	S	X	N	Z	V	C	Operation Performed
Register-Register Move	MOVE.B	sDn,dDn	2	4(1/0)				×	×	0	0	[dDn<07>] ← [sDn<0-7>] Move one byte of any data register to any data register. Bits 8-31 of the destination register are not affected.
	MOVE.W	rs,Dn	2	4(1/0)				×	×	0	0	[Dn<0-15>] ← [rs<0-15>] Move one word of any data or address register to any data register. Bits 16-31 of the destination register are not affected.
	MOVE.W	rs,An	2	4(1/0)								[An<015>] ← [rs<0-15>] [An<16-31>] ← [An<15>] Move one word of any data or address register to any address register. The sign is extended to all upper bits of the address register.
	MOVE.L	rs,Dn	2	4(1/0)				×	×	0	0	[Dn<0-31>] ← [rs<0-31>] Move the contents of any data or address register to any data register.
	MOVE.L	rs,An	2	4(1/0)								[An<0-31>] ← [rs<0-31>] Move the contents of any data or address register to any address register.
Register-Register Operate	ABCD	sDn,dDn	2	6(1/0)			×	U	U	U	×	[dDn<0-7>] ← [dDn<0-7>] + [sDn<0-7>] + X Add decimal source data register byte to destination data register byte with carry (Extend bit). Bits 8-31 of the destination data register are not affected.
	ADD.B	sDn,dDn	2	4(1/0)			×	×	×	×	×	[dDn<0-7>] ← [dDn<0-7>] + [sDn<0-7>] Add byte from data registers to data register. Bits 8-31 of the destination data register are not affected.
	ADD.W	rs,Dn	2	4(1/0)			×	×	×	×	×	[Dn<0-15>] ← [Dn<0-15>] + [rs<0-15>] Add word from source register to data register. Bits 16-31 of the destination data register are not affected.
	ADD.W	rs,An	2	8(1/0)								[An<0-15>] ← [An<0-15>] + [rs<0-15>] (sign extended) Add word from source register to address register. The sign of the source word is extended to a full 32 bits for the operation.
	ADD.L	rs,Dn	2	8(1/0)			×	×	×	×	×	[Dn<0-31>] ← [Dn<0-31>] + [rs<0-31>] Add long word from source register to data register.
	ADD.L	rs,An	2	8(1/0)								[An<0-31>] ← [An<0-31>] + rs<0-31>] Add long word from source register to address register.
	ADDX.B	sDn,dDn	2	4(1/0)			×	×	×	×	×	[dDn<0-7>] ← [dDn<0-7] + [sDn<0-7>] + X Add source data register byte to destination data register byte with carry (Extend bit). Bits 8-31 of the destination data register are not affected.
	ADDX.W	sDn, dDn	2	4(1/0)			×	×	×	×	×	[dDn<0-15>] ← [dDn<0-15>] + [sDn<0-15>] + X Add source data register word to destination data register word with carry (Extend bit). Bits 16-31 of the destination data register are not affected.
	ADDX.L	sDn,dDn	2	8(1/0)			×	×	×	×	×	[dDn<0-31>] ← [dDn<0-31>] + [sDn<0-31>] + X Add source data register long word to destination data register long word with carry (Extend bit).
	AND.B	sDn,dDn	2	4(1/0)				×	×	0	0	[dDn<0-7>] ← [dDn<0-7>] ∧ [sDn<0-7>] AND byte from data register to data register. Bits 8-31 of the destination data register are not affected.

Table A-2. MC68000 Instruction Set Summary (Continued)

Mnemonic	Operand(s)	Bytes	Clock Cycles	T	S	X	N	Z	V	C	Operation Performed
AND.W	sDn,dDn	2	4(1/0)				X	X	0	0	[dDn<0-15>] ← [dDn<0-15>] ∧ [sDn<0-15>] AND word from data register to data register. Bits 16-31 of the destination data register are not affected.
AND.L	sDn,dDn	2	8(1/0)				X	X	0	0	[dDn<0-31>] ← [dDn<0-31>] ∧ [sDn<0-31>] AND long word from data register to data register.
CMP.B	sDn,dDn	2	4(1/0)				X	X	X	X	[dDn<0-7>] − [sDn<0-7>] Compare data register bytes and set condition codes accordingly. Register data are not changed on any compares.
CMP.W	rs,Dn	2	4(1/0)				X	X	X	X	[Dn<0-15>] − [rs<0-15>] Compare data register word with register word and set condition codes accordingly.
CMP.W	rs,An	2	6(1/0)				X	X	X	X	[An<0-15>] − [rs<0-15>] Compare address register word with register word and set condition codes accordingly.
CMP.L	rs,Dn	2	6(1/0)				X	X	X	X	[Dn<0-31>] − [rs<0-31>] Compare data register with register and set condition codes accordingly.
CMP.L	rs,An	2	6(1/0)				X	X	X	X	[An<0-31>] − [rs<0-31>] Compare address register with register and set condition codes accordingly.
DIVS	sDn,dDn	2	≤158(1/0)				X	X	X	0	[dDn<0-15>] ← [dDn<0-31>] ÷ [sDn<0-15>] [dDn<016-31>] ← remainder Divide signed numbers. Division by zero causes a TRAP.
DIVU	sDn,dDn	2	≤140(1/0)				X	X	X	0	[dDn<0-15>] ← [dDn<0-31>] ÷ [sDn<0-15>] [dDn<16-31>] ← remainder Divide unsigned numbers. Division by zero causes a TRAP.
EOR.B	sDn,dDn	2	4(1/0)				X	X	0	0	[dDn<0-7>] ← [dDn<0-7>] ⊻ [sDn<0-7>] Exclusive-OR byte from data register to data register. Bits 8-31 of the destination data register are not affected.
EOR.W	sDn,dDn	2	4(1/0)				X	X	0	0	[dDn<0-15>] ← [dDn<0-15>] ⊻ [sDn<0-15>] Exclusive-OR word from data register to data register. Bits 16-31 of the destination data register are not affected.
EOR.L	sDn,dDn	2	8(1/0)				X	X	0	0	[dDn<0-31>] ← [dDn<0-31>] ⊻ [sDn<0-31>] Exclusive-OR long word from data register to data register.
EXG	rs,rd	2	6(1/0)								[rd] ⟶ [rs] Exchange the contents of two registers. This is always a long word operation.
MULS	sDn,dDn	2	≤70(1/0)				X	X	0	0	[dDn<0-31>] ← [dDn<0-15>] × [sDn<0-15>] Multiply two 16-bit signed numbers, yielding a 32-bit signed product.
MULU	sDn,dDn	2	≤70(1/0)				X	X	0	0	[dDn<0-31>] ← [dDn<0-15>] × [sDn<0-15>] Multiply two 16-bit unsigned numbers, yielding a 32-bit unsigned product.
OR.B	sDn,dDn	2	4(1/0)				X	X	0	0	[dDn<0-7>] ← [dDn<0-7>] ∨ [sDn<0-7>] OR byte from data register to data register. Bits 8-31 of the destination dat register are not affected.

Register-Register Operate (Continued)

Table A-2. MC68000 Instruction Set Summary (Continued)

Mnemonic	Operand(s)	Bytes	Clock Cycles	T	S	X	N	Z	V	C	Operation Performed
OR.W	sDn,dDn	2	4(1/0)				X	X	0	0	[dDn<0-15>] ← [dDn<0-15>] ∨ [sDn<0-15>] OR word from data register to data register. Bits 16-31 of the destination data register are not affected.
OR.L	sDn,dDn	2	8(1/0)				X	X	0	0	[dDn<0-31>] ← [dDn<0-31>] ∨ [sDn<0-31>] OR long word from data register to data register.
SBCD	sDn,dDn	2	6(1/0)			X	U	U	U	X	[dDn<0-7>] ← [dDn<0-7>] − [sDn<0-7>] − X Subtract decimal source data register byte from destination data register byte with carry (Extend bit). Bits 8-31 of the destination data register are not affected.
SUB.B	sDn,dDn	2	4(1/0)			X	X	X	X	X	[dDn<0-7>] ← [dDn<0-7>] − [sDn<0-7>] Subtract data register bytes. Bits 8-31 of the destination data register bytes are not affected.
SUB.W	rs,Dn	2	4(1/0)			X	X	X	X	X	[Dn<0-15>] ← [Dn<0-15>] − [rs<0-15>] Subtract register words. Bits 16-31 of the destination data register are not affected.
SUB.W	rs,An	2	8(1/0)								[An<0-15>] ← [An<0-15>] − [rs<0-15>] (sign extended) Subtract source register word from address register. The sign of the source word is extended to a full 32 bits for the operation.
SUB.L	rs,Dn	2	8(1/0)			X	X	X	X	X	[Dn<0-31>] ← [Dn<0-31>] − [rs<0-31>] Subtract source register long word from data register.
SUB.L	rs,An	2	8(1/0)								[An<0-31>] ← [An<0-31>] − [rs<0-31>] Subtract source register long word from address register.
SUBX.B	sDn,dDn	2	4(1/0)			X	X	X	X	X	[dDn<0-7>] ← [dDn<0-7>] − [sDn<0-7>] − X Subtract source data register byte from destination data register byte with borrow (Extend bit). Bits 8-31 of the destination data register are not affected.
SUBX.W	sDn,dDn	2	4(1/0)			X	X	X	X	X	[dDn<0-15>] ← [dDn<0-15>] − [sDn<0-15>] − X Subtract source data register word from destination data register word with borrow (Extend bit). Bits 16-31 of the destination data registers are not affected.
SUBX.L	sDn,dDn	2	8(1/0)			X	X	X	X	X	[dDn<0-31>] ← [dDn<0-31>] − [sDn<0-31>] − X Subtract source data register long word from destination data register long word with borrow (Extend bit).
CLR.B	Dn	2	4(1/0)				0	1	0	0	[Dn<0-7>] ← 0 Clear data register byte to zeroes. Bits 8-31 of the data register are not affected.
CLR.W	Dn	2	4(1/0)				0	1	0	0	[Dn<0-15>] ← 0 Clear data register word to zeroes. Bits 16-31 of the data register are not affected.
CLR.L	Dn	2	6(1/0)				0	1	0	0	[Dn<0-31>] ← 0 Clear data register to zeroes
EXT.W	Dn	2	4(1/0)				X	X	0	0	[Dn<8-15>] ← [Dn<7>] Extend sign bit of data byte to data word size. Bits 16-31 of the data register are not affected.
EXT.L	Dn	2	4(1/0)				X	X	0	0	[Dn<16-31>] ← [Dn<15>] Extend sign bit of data word to long data word size.

Groups: Register-Register Operate (Continued); Register Operate

Table A-2. MC68000 Instruction Set Summary (Continued)

Mnemonic	Operand(s)	Bytes	Clock Cycles	T	S	X	N	Z	V	C	Operation Performed
NBCD	Dn	2	6(1/0)			X	U	X	U	X	[Dn<0-7>] — [Dn<0-7>] — X. Negate decimal register byte. Bits 8-31 of the data register are not affected.
NEG.B	Dn	2	4(1/0)			X	X	X	X	X	[Dn<0-7>] — 0 — [Dn<0-7>]. Negate register byte. Bits 8-31 of the data register are not affected.
NEG.W	Dn	2	4(1/0)			X	X	X	X	X	[Dn<0-15>] — 0 — [Dn<0-15>]. Negate register word. Bits 16-31 of the data register are not affected.
NEG.L	Dn	2	6(1/0)			X	X	X	X	X	[Dn<0-31>] — 0 — [Dn<0-31>]. Negate register long word.
NEG.B	Dn	2	4(1/0)			X	X	X	X	X	[Dn<0-7>] — 0 — [Dn<0-7>] — X. Negate register byte with Extend. Bits 8-31 of the data register are not affected.
NEG.W	Dn	2	4(1/0)			X	X	X	X	X	[Dn<0-15>] — 0 — [Dn<0-15>] — X. Negate register word with Extend. Bits 16-31 of the data register are not affected.
NEG.L	Dn	2	6(1/0)			X	X	X	X	X	[Dn<0-31>] — 0 — [Dn<0-31>] — X. Negate register long word with Extend.
NOT.B	Dn	2	4(1/0)				X	X	0	0	[Dn<0-7>] — [Dn<0-7>]. Ones complement data register byte. Bits 8-31 of the data register are not affected.
NOT.W	Dn	2	6(1/0)				X	X	0	0	[Dn<0-15>] — [Dn<0-15>]. Ones complement data register word. Bits 16-31 of the data register are not affected.
NOT.L	Dn	2	6(1/0)				X	X	0	0	[Dn<0-31>] — [Dn<0-31>]. Ones complement data register contents.
Scc	Dn	2	9(1/1)								[Dn<0-7>] — all 1's if cc = TRUE; [Dn<0-7>] — all 0's if cc = FALSE. Set status in data register byte.
SWAP	Dn	2	4(1/0)				X	X	0	0	[Dn<0-15>] —— [Dn<16-31>]. Exchange the two 16-bit halves of a data register.
TAS	Dn	2	4(1/0)				X	X	0	0	[Dn<7>] — 1. Test status of data register byte and set bit 7 to 1.
TST.B	Dn	2	4(1/0)				X	X	0	0	[Dn<0-7>] — 0. Test status of data register byte. The data register contents are not changed.
TST.W	Dn	2	4(1/0)				X	X	0	0	[Dn<0-15>] — 0. Test status of data register word. The data register contents are not changed.
TST.L	Dn	2	4(1/0)				X	X	0	0	[Dn<0-31>] — 0. Test status of data register long word. The data register contents are not changed.

Register-Register Operate (Continued)

Table A-2. MC68000 Instruction Set Summary (Continued)

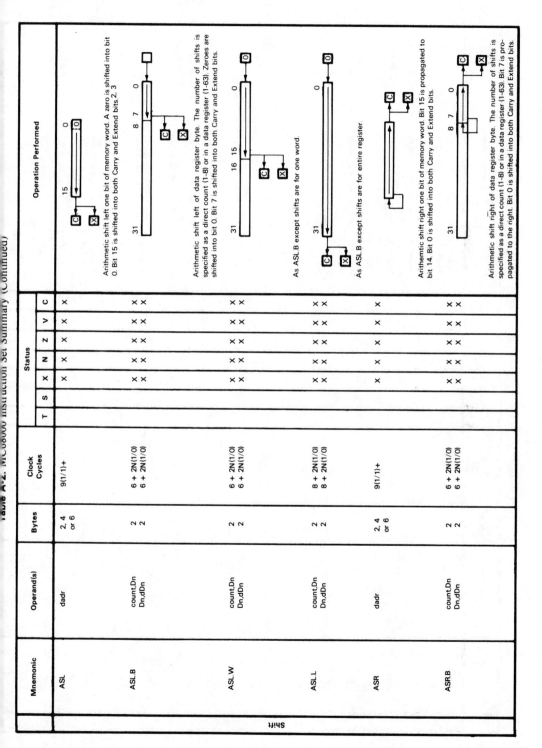

Mnemonic	Operand(s)	Bytes	Clock Cycles	T	S	X	N	Z	V	C	Operation Performed
ASL	dadr	2, 4 or 6	9(1/1)+			X	X	X	X	X	Arithmetic shift left one bit of memory word. A zero is shifted into bit 0. Bit 15 is shifted into both Carry and Extend bits.[2],[3]
ASL.B	count,Dn Dn,dDn	2 2	6 + 2N(1/0) 6 + 2N(1/0)			X X	X X	X X	X X	X X	Arithmetic shift left of data register byte. The number of shifts is specified as a direct count (1-8) or in a data register (1-63). Zeroes are shifted into bit 0. Bit 7 is shifted into both Carry and Extend bits.
ASL.W	count,Dn Dn,dDn	2 2	6 + 2N(1/0) 6 + 2N(1/0)			X X	X X	X X	X X	X X	As ASL.B except shifts are for one word.
ASL.L	count,Dn Dn,dDn	2 2	8 + 2N(1/0) 8 + 2N(1/0)			X X	X X	X X	X X	X X	As ASL.B except shifts are for entire register.
ASR	dadr	2, 4 or 6	9(1/1)+			X	X	X	X	X	Arithmetic shift right one bit of memory word. Bit 15 is propagated to bit 14. Bit 0 is shifted into both Carry and Extend bits.
ASR.B	count,Dn Dn,dDn	2 2	6 + 2N(1/0) 6 + 2N(1/0)			X X	X X	X X	X X	X X	Arithemtic shift right of data register byte. The number of shifts is specified as a direct count (1-8) or in a data register (1-63). Bit 7 is pro-pagated to the right. Bit 0 is shifted into both Carry and Extend bits.

Shift

Table A-2. MC68000 Instruction Set Summary (Continued)

Mnemonic	Operand(s)	Bytes	Clock Cycles	T	S	X	N	Z	V	C	Operation Performed
ASR.W	count,Dn Dn,dDn	2 2	6 + 2N(1/0) 6 + 2N(1/0)			X X	X X	X X	X X	X X	As ASR.B except shifts are for one word.
ASR.L	count,Dn Dn,dDn	2 2	8 + 2N(1/0) 8 + 2N(1/0)			X X	X X	X X	X X	X X	As ASR.B except shifts are for entire register.
LSL	dadr	2, 4 or 6	9(1/1)+			X	X	X	0	X	Logical shift left one bit of memory word. A zero is shifted into bit 0. Bit 15 is shifted into both Carry and Extend bits. (Note that LSL is identical to ASL except for the Overflow condition.)[2,3]
LSL.B	count,Dn Dn,dDn	2 2	6 + 2N(1/0) 6 + 2N(1/0)			X X	X X	X X	0 0	X X	Logical shift left of data register byte. The number of shifts is specified as a direct count (1–8) or in a data register (1–63). Zeroes are shifted into bit 0. Bit 7 is shifted into both Carry and Extend bits.
LSL.W	count,Dn Dn,dDn	2 2	6 + 2N(1/0) 6 + 2N(1/0)			X X	X X	X X	0 0	X X	As LSL.B except shifts are for one word.
LSL.L	count,Dn Dn,dDn	2	8 + 2N(1/0) 8 + 2N(1/0)			X X	X X	X X	0 0	X X	As LSL.B except shifts are for entire register.

Shift (Continued)

Table A-2. MC68000 Instruction Set Summary (Continued)

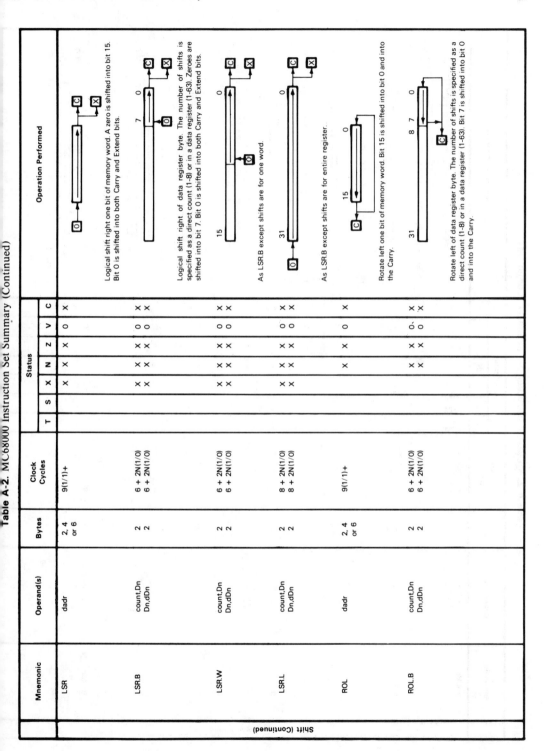

Mnemonic	Operand(s)	Bytes	Clock Cycles	T	S	Status X	N	Z	V	C	Operation Performed
LSR	dadr	2, 4 or 6	9(1/1)+			X	X	X	0	X	Logical shift right one bit of memory word. A zero is shifted into bit 15. Bit 0 is shifted into both Carry and Extend bits.
LSR.B	count,Dn Dn,dDn	2 2	6 + 2N(1/0) 6 + 2N(1/0)			X X	X X	X X	0 0	X X	Logical shift right of data register byte. The number of shifts is specified as a direct count (1–8) or in a data register (1–63). Zeroes are shifted into bit 7. Bit 0 is shifted into both Carry and Extend bits.
LSR.W	count,Dn Dn,dDn	2 2	6 + 2N(1/0) 6 + 2N(1/0)			X X	X X	X X	0 0	X X	As LSR.B except shifts are for one word.
LSR.L	count,Dn Dn,dDn	2 2	8 + 2N(1/0) 8 + 2N(1/0)			X X	X X	X X	0 0	X X	As LSR.B except shifts are for entire register.
ROL	dadr	2, 4 or 6	9(1/1)+				X	X	0	X	Rotate left one bit of memory word. Bit 15 is shifted into bit 0 and into the Carry.
ROL.B	count,Dn Dn,dDn	2 2	6 + 2N(1/0) 6 + 2N(1/0)				X X	X X	0 0	X X	Rotate left of data register byte. The number of shifts is specified as a direct count (1–8) or in a data register (1–63). Bit 7 is shifted into bit 0 and into the Carry.

Shift (Continued)

Table A-2. MC68000 Instruction Set Summary (Continued)

Shift (Continued)

Mnemonic	Operand(s)	Bytes	Clock Cycles	T	S	X	N	Z	V	C	Operation Performed
ROL.W	count,Dn Dn,dDn	2 2	6 + 2N(1/0) 6 + 2N(1/0)			x x	x x	x x	o o	x x	As ROL.B except shifts are for one word.
ROL.L	count,Dn Dn,dDn	2 2	8 + 2N(1/0) 8 + 2N(1/0)			x x	x x	x x	o o	x x	As ROL.B except shifts are for entire register.
ROR	dadr	2, 4 or 6	9(1/1)+				x	x	o	x	Rotate right one bit of memory word. Bit 0 is shifted into bit 15 and into the Carry.
RORB	count,Dn Dn,dDn	2 2	6 + 2N(1/0) 6 + 2N(1/0)			x x	x x	x x	o o	x x	Rotate right of data register byte. The number of shifts is specified as a direct count (1-8) or in a data register (1-63). Bit 0 is shifted into bit 7 and into the Carry.
ROR.W	count,Dn Dn,dDn	2 2	6 + 2N(1/0) 6 + 2N(1/0)			x x	x x	x x	o o	x x	As ROR.B except shifts are for one word.
RORL	count,Dn Dn,dDn	2 2	8 + 2N(1/0) 8 + 2N(1/0)			x x	x x	x x	o o	x x	As ROR.B except shifts are for entire register.
ROXL	dadr	2, 4 or 6	9(1/1)+			x	x	x	o	x	Rotate left one bit of memory word and Extend one bit. Bit 15 is shifted into both Extend and Carry bits. The Extend bit is shifted into bit 0.

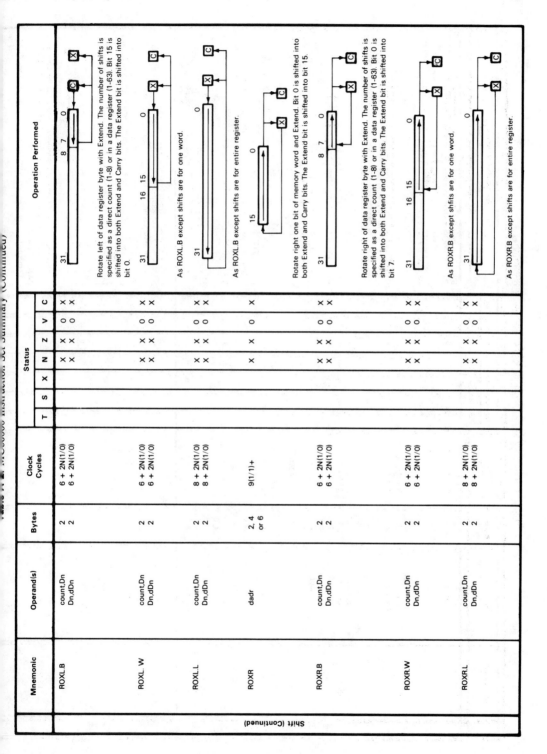

Table A.1 M68000 Instruction Set Summary (Continued)

Mnemonic	Operand(s)	Bytes	Clock Cycles	Status							Operation Performed
				T	S	X	N	Z	V	C	
ROXL.B	count,Dn Dn,dDn	2 2	6 + 2N(1/0) 6 + 2N(1/0)				X X	X X	O O	X X	Rotate left of data register byte with Extend. The number of shifts is specified as a direct count (1-8) or in a data register (1-63). Bit 15 is shifted into both Extend and Carry bits. The Extend bit is shifted into bit 0.
ROXL.W	count,Dn Dn,dDn	2 2	6 + 2N(1/0) 6 + 2N(1/0)				X X	X X	O O	X X	As ROXL.B except shifts are for one word.
ROXL.L	count,Dn Dn,dDn	2 2	8 + 2N(1/0) 8 + 2N(1/0)				X X	X X	O O	X X	As ROXL.B except shifts are for entire register.
ROXR	dadr	2, 4 or 6	9(1/1)+				X	X	O	X	Rotate right one bit of memory word and Extend. Bit 0 is shifted into both Extend and Carry bits. The Extend bit is shifted into bit 15.
ROXR.B	count,Dn Dn,dDn	2 2	6 + 2N(1/0) 6 + 2N(1/0)				X X	X X	O O	X X	Rotate right of data register byte with Extend. The number of shifts is specified as a direct count (1-8) or in a data register (1-63). Bit 0 is shifted into both Extend and Carry bits. The Extend bit is shifted into bit 7.
ROXR.W	count,Dn Dn,dDn	2 2	6 + 2N(1/0) 6 + 2N(1/0)				X X	X X	O O	X X	As ROXR.B except shifts are for one word.
ROXR.L	count,Dn Dn,dDn	2 2	8 + 2N(1/0) 8 + 2N(1/0)				X X	X X	O O	X X	As ROXR.B except shifts are for entire register.

Shift (Continued)

Table A-2. MC68000 Instruction Set Summary (Continued)

	Mnemonic	Operand(s)	Bytes	Clock Cycles	T	S	X	N	Z	V	C	Operation Performed
Bit Manipulation	BTST	bit,Dn Dn,dDn	4 2	10(2/0) 6(1/0)					X X			[Z] ← [Dn<bit>] [Z] ← [dDn<[Dn]>] Test a bit of a data register and reflect status in Zero bit. The bit to be tested may be specified directly or in a data register (bit 0-31 in either case).
	BTST	bitb,dadr Dn,dadr	4, 6 or 8 2, 4 or 6	8(2/0)+ 4(1/0)+					X X			[Z] ← [dadr<bitb>] [Z] ← [dadr<[Dn]>] Test a bit of a memory byte and reflect status in Zero bit. The bit to be tested may be specified directly or in a data register (bit 0-7 in either case).[1]
	BSET	bit,Dn Dn,dDn bitb,dadr Dn,dadr	4 2 4, 6 or 8 2, 4 or 6	12(2/0) 8(1/0) 13(2/1)+ 9(1/1)+					X X X X			[Z] ← [Dn<bit>], [Dn<bit>] ← 1 [Z] ← [dDn<[Dn]>], [dDn<[Dn]>] ← 1 [Z] ← [dadr<bitb>], [dadr<bitb>] ← 1 [Z] ← [dadr<[Dn]>], [dadr<[Dn]>] ← 1 Test a bit as (BTST) and then set the specified bit.
	BCLR	bit,Dn Dn,dDn bitb,dadr Dn,dadr	4 2 4, 6 or 8 2, 4 or 6	14(2/0) 8(1/0) 13(2/1)+ 9(1/1)+					X X X X			[Z] ← [Dn<bit>], [Dn<bit>] ← 0 [Z] ← [dDn<[Dn]>], [dDn<[Dn]>] ← 0 [Z] ← [dadr<bit b>], [dadr<bit b>] ← 0 [Z] ← [dadr<[Dn]>], [dadr<[Dn]>] ← 0 Test a bit (as BTST) and then clear the specified bit.
	BCHG	bit,Dn Dn,dDn bitb,dadr Dn,dadr	4 2 4, 6 or 8 2, 4 or 6	12(2/0) 8(1/0) 13(2/1) 9(1/1)					X X X X			[Z] ← [dadr<bitl>], [dadr<bitl>] ← [Dn<bitl>] [Z] ← [dDn<[Dn]>], [dDn<[Dn]>], [dDn<[dDn]>] [Z] ← [dadr<bitb>], [dadr<bitb>] ← [dadr<bitb>] [Z] ← [dadr<[Dn]>], [dadr<[Dn]>] ← [dadr<[Dn]>] Test a bit (as BTST) and then complement the specified bit.
Stack	MOVE	An,USP	2	4(1/0)								[USP] ← [An] Move contents of address register to User Stack Pointer. **This is a privileged instruction.**
	MOVE	USP,An	2	4(1/0)								[An] ← [USP] Move contents of User Stack Pointer to address register. **This is a privileged instruction.**
	LINK	An,d16	4	18(2/2)								[A7] ← [A7] − 2 [[A7]] ← [An] [An] ← [A7] [A7] ← [A7] + d16 Save the contents of the specified address register on the Stack, load the current Stack Pointer to the specified address register, and set the Stack Pointer to point beyond the temporary stack storage area.
	PEA	jadr	2, 4 or 6	10(1/2)+								[A7] ← [A7] − 2 [[A7]] ← jadr Compute long word address and push address onto the Stack.[3]

Table A-2. MC68000 Instruction Set Summary (Continued)

	Mnemonic	Operand(s)	Bytes	Clock Cycles	T	S	X	N	Z	V	C	Operation Performed
Stack (Cont)	UWLK	An	2	12(3/0)								[A7] ← [An] [An] ← [[A7]] [A7] ← [A7] + 2 Store the contents of the specified address register to the Stack Pointer (A7) and load the specified address register from the stack.
Interrupt and Trap	CHK	data16,Dn	4	49(6/3), 12(2/0)				X	U	U	U	If [Dn<0-15>] < 0 or [Dn<0-15>] > data16 then [PC] ← CHK interrupt vector
	CHK	Dn,dDn	2	45(5/3), 8(1/0)				X	U	U	U	If [dDn<0-15>] < 0 or [dDn<0-15>] > [Dn<0-15>] then [PC] ← CHK interrupt vector
	CHK	sadr,Dn	2, 4 or 6	45(5/3), 8(1/0)				X	U	U	U	If [Dn<0-15>] < 0 or [Dn<0-15>] > [sadr] then [PC] ← CHK interrupt vector Check register against bounds and initiate Check interrupt processing if register word is out of bounds. The upper bound is a twos complement integer specified as immediate data, in a data register, or in a memory word.2, 3
	TRAP	vector	2	37(4/3)								[A7] ← [A7] - 2 [[A7]] ← [PC] [A7] ← [A7] - 2 [[A7]] ← [SR] [PC] ← vector Initiate exception processing through specified vector.
	TRAPV		2	37(5/3), 4(1/0)			X	X	X	X	X	If Overflow = 1 then TRAP Initiate exception processing through Overflow vector if the Overflow bit is on.
	RTE		2	20(5/0)	X	X	X	X	X	X	X	[SR] ← [[A7]], [A7] ← [A7] + 2 [PC] ← [[A7]], [A7] ← [A7] + 2 Return from exception.
Status	MOVE	Dn,CCr	2	12(2/0)			X	X	X	X	X	[SR<0-4>] ← [Dn<0-4>] Move status data from data register to condition codes.
	MOVE	sadr,CCR	2, 4 or 6	12(2/0)+			X	X	X	X	X	[SR<0-4>] ← [sadr<0-4>] Move status data from memory location to condition codes. The source address is a word address.2, 3
	MOVE	data8,CCR	4	16(3/0)			X	X	X	X	X	[SR<0-4>] ← data8<0-4> Move immediate status data to condition codes.
	MOVE	Dn,SR	2	12(2/0)	X	X	X	X	X	X	X	[SR] ← [Dn<0-15>] Moves status word from data register to Status register. This is a privileged instruction.
	MOVE	sadr,SR	2, 4 or 6	12(2/0)+	X	X	X	X	X	X	X	[SR] ← [sadr] Move status word from memory location to Status register. The source address is a word address.2, 3
	MOVE	data16,SR	4	16(3/0)	X	X	X	X	X	X	X	[SR] ← data16 Move immediate status word to Status register. This is a privileged instruction.
	MOVE	SR,Dn	2	6(1/0)								[Dn<0-15>] ← [SR] Move contents of Status register to data register. Bits 16-31 of the data register are not affected.

Table A-2. MC68000 Instruction Set Summary (Continued)

Group	Mnemonic	Operand(s)	Bytes	Clock Cycles	T	S	X	N	Z	V	C	Operation Performed
Status (Continued)	MOVE	SR,dadr	2, 4 or 6	9(1/1)+								[dadr] → [SR] Move contents of Status register to memory location. The destination address is a word address. 2, 3
	AND.B	data8,SR	4	20(3/0)		X	X	X	X	X	X	[SR<0-7>] → [SR<0-7>] ∧ data8 AND immediate data byte to low-order Status register byte.
	AND.W	data16,SR	4	20(3/0)	X	X	X	X	X	X	X	[SR] → [SR] ∧ data16 AND immediate data with Status register. **This is a privileged instruction.**
	EOR.B	data8,SR	4	20(3/0)		X	X	X	X	X	X	[SR<0-7>] → [SR<0-7>] ⊻ data8 Exclusive-OR immediate data byte to low-order Status register byte.
	EOR.W	data16,SR	4	20(3/0)	X	X	X	X	X	X	X	[SR] → [SR] ⊻ data16 Exclusive-OR immediate data with Status register. **This is a privileged instruction.**
	OR.B	data8,SR	4	20(3/0)		X	X	X	X	X	X	[SR<0-7>] → [SR<0-7>] ∧ data8 OR immediate data byte to low-order Status register byte.
	OR.W	data16,SR	4	20(3/0)	X	X	X	X	X	X	X	[SR] → [SR] ∨ data16 OR immediate data with Status register. **This is a privileged instruction.**
Miscellaneous Control	NOP		2	4(1/0)								No operation.
	RESET		2	132(1/0)								Reset. **This is a privileged instruction.**
	STOP	data16	4	8(2/0)			X	X	X	X	X	[SR] → data16 Stop processor. **This is a privileged instruction.**

B

Instruction Object Code Tables

The object code for each MC68000 instruction is shown alphabetically by instruction mnemonic in Table B-1. The object codes are listed in numerical order in Table B-2.

For instruction words which have no variations, object codes are represented as four hexadecimal digits; for example, 4E71.

For instruction words with variation in one of the two bytes, the object code is shown as a combination of lower case variables, hex digits, and binary digits. Each byte of an instruction word in Tables B-1 and B-2 is subdivided into two "nibble" fields (1 nibble = 4 bits). If a single digit appears in a nibble field, it is a hexadecimal digit. If four digits, or a combination of digits and lower-case variables (for example, 1rrr), appear in a nibble field, each digit represents a single bit.

Note that some lower-case variables are used to represent hexadecimal digits rather than binary digits. When four of these hexadecimal variable characters (for example xxxx or yyyy) are used to represent a 16-bit word, they will appear grouped together in the center of the 2-byte column comprising that word.

INSTRUCTION EXECUTION TIMES

Table B-1 lists the instruction execution time in clock cycles. Each cycle = 125 nanoseconds (when $f_{CLK} = 8.0$ MHz).

The abbreviations and notations used in the "clock cycles" column are
defined as follows:

+ea   Effective address overhead. This is the additional time
                           required to execute the instruction for addressing modes
                           that take longer to execute than the nominal register
                           indirect address. The following are the additional clock
                           cycles required:

Addressing Mode	Additional Clock Cycles
(An)	0
(An)+	0
−(An)	2
d16(An)	5
d8(An,i)	7
addr-16-bit	5
addr-32-bit	10
label	5
label(i)	7

N   For shift instructions, the number of shifts. For move multi-
                           ple instructions, the number of registers being moved.

*   The first value is for branch or trap taken, the second is for
                           branch or trap not taken. In the case of Bcc, the first of
                           the latter numbers is for a two-byte instruction (8-bit dis-
                           placement), and the second is for a four-byte instruction
                           (16-bit displacement). In the case of DBcc, the first of the
                           latter numbers is for branch not taken due to condition
                           true, and the second is for branch not taken due to
                           counter timeout.

**   Indicates maximum value.

***   The lower value is for condition false (byte set to all ones),
                           the higher value is for condition true (byte cleared to all
                           zeroes).

The following abbreviations are used in Tables B-1 and B-2:

a   Operand addressing mode (1 bit)
                               0 = data register to data register
                               1 = memory to memory

bbb   3 bits of immediate data. In bit operations the bit numbers
                               0 - 7.

bbbbb   Bit numbers 0 - 31.

ccc   Shift count 000 = 8 shifts
                               001 = 1 shift
                               010 = 2 shifts
                               011 = 3 shifts
                               100 = 4 shifts
                               101 = 5 shifts
                               110 = 6 shifts
                               111 = 7 shifts

ddd   Destination register — same coding as rrr.

eeeee   Source effective address (6 bits)

Addressing Mode	Mode/Register	[EXT]
(An)	010rrr	---
(An)+	011rrr	---
-(An)	100rrr	---
d16(An)	101rrr	xxxx
d8(An,i)	110rrr	a iii w 000 xx
addr-16-bit	111000	pppp
addr-32-bit	111001	pppp qqqq
label	111010	xxxx
label(i)	111011	a iii w 000 xx

[EXT]   One or two optional words of extension addressing that may or may not appear, depending on the addressing mode (see the Addressing Modes description).

ffffff   Destination effective address — same as eeeeee except no label or label(i).

gggggg   Destination effective address but in a format with the MODE and REGISTER fields switched (e.g., (An)=rrr010).

hhhhhh   Multiple-destination effective address — same as ffffff except no (An)+ or -(An).?

iii   Index register — same coding as rrr.

jjjjjj   Jump effective address — same as eeeeee except no (An)+ or -(An).

kkkk   Register mask list for predecrement mode, in the following format (a "1" selects the register):

15 14 13 12 11 10 9 8 7 6 5 4 3 2 1 0
D0 D1 D2 D3 D4 D5 D6 D7 A0 A1 A2 A3 A4 A5 A6 A7

mmmm   Register mask list for non-predecrement modes, in the format (a "1" selects the register):

15 14 13 12 11 10 9 8 7 6 5 4 3 2 1 0
A7 A6 A5 A4 A3 A2 A1 A0 D7 D6 D5 D4 D3 D2 D1 D0

pppp   16-bit address word or most significant word of 32-bit address

qqqq   Least significant word of 32-bit address

rrr   Register.   000 = D0 or A0
001 = D1 or A1
010 = D2 or A2
011 = D3 or A3
100 = D4 or A4
101 = D5 or A5
110 = D6 or A6
111 = D7 or A7

sss   Source register — same coding as rrr.

t   Type of Register.   0 = Dn
1 = An

vvvv   4-bit vector

w   Index size. 0 = sign extended, low-order integer in index register
1 = long word value in Index register

xx   8-bit address displacement

xxxx   16-bit address displacement

yy   8-bit immediate data

yyyy   16-bit immediate data or most significant word of 32-bit data

zzzz   Least significant word of 32-bit data

Table B-1. MC68000 Instruction Object Codes

Instruction	Byte 1	Byte 2	Byte 3	Byte 4	Byte 5	Byte 6	Byte 7	Byte 8	Byte 9	Byte 10	Bytes	Clock Cycles
ABCD												
−(SAn),−(dAn)	C ddd1	0 1sss									2	19(3/1)
sDn,dDn	C ddd1	0 0sss									2	6(1/0)
ADD.B												
data8,dadr	0 6	00ff ffff	00	yy	[EXT]						4, 6, or 8	13(2/1)+
data8,Dn	0 6	0 0ddd	00	yy							4	8(2/0)
Dn,dadr	D ddd1	00ff ffff	[EXT]								2, 4, or 6	9(1/1)+
sadr,Dn	D ddd0	00ee eeee	[EXT]								2, 4, or 6	4(1/0)+
sDn,dDn	D ddd0	00ee eeee									2	4(1/0)
ADD.L												
data32,An	D ddd1	F C	yyyy		zzzz						6	16(3/0)
data32,dadr	0 6	10ff ffff	yyyy		zzzz		[EXT]		[EXT]		6, 8, or 10	22(3/2)+
data32,Dn	0 6	8 0ddd	yyyy		zzzz						6	16(3/0)
Dn,dadr	D ddd1	10ff ffff	[EXT]								2, 4, or 6	14(1/2)+
rs,An	D ddd1	C tsss									2	8(1/0)
rs,Dn	D ddd0	8 tsss									2	6(1/0)+
sadr,An	D ddd1	11ee eeee	[EXT]								2, 4, or 6	6(1/0)+
sadr,Dn	D ddd0	10ee eeee	[EXT]								2, 4, or 6	8(2/0)
ADD.W												
data16,An	D ddd0	F C	yyyy		[EXT]						4	13(2/1)
data16,dadr	0 6	01ff ffff	yyyy		[EXT]						4, 6, or 8	8(2/0)
Dn,dadr	D ddd1	01ff ffff	[EXT]								2, 4, or 6	9(1/1)+
rs,An	D ddd0	C tsss									2	8(1/0)
rs,Dn	D ddd0	4 tsss									2	4(1/0)
ADDQ.B												
data3,dadr	5 bbb0	00ff ffff	[EXT]								2, 4, or 6	8(1/0)+
data3,Dn	5 bbb0	0 0ddd									2	4(1/0)+
ADDQ.L												
data3,An	5 bbb0	8 1ddd									2	9(1/0)+
data3,dadr	5 bbb0	10ff ffff	[EXT]								2, 4, or 6	4(1/0)
data3,Dn	5 bbb0	8 0ddd									2	8(1/0)
ADDQ.W												
data3,An	5 bbb0	4 1ddd									2	14(1/2)+
data3,dadr	5 bbb0	01ff ffff	[EXT]								2, 4, or 6	8(1/0)
data3,Dn	5 bbb0	4 0ddd									2	4(1/0)
ADDX.B												
−(sAn),−(dAn)	D ddd1	0 1sss									2	19(3/1)
sDn,dDn	D ddd1	0 0sss									2	4(1/0)
ADDX.L												
−(sAn),−(dAn)	D ddd1	8 1sss									2	32(5/2)
SDn,dDn	D ddd1	8 0sss									2	8(1/0)
ADDX.W												
−(sAn),−(dAn)	D ddd1	4 1sss									2	19(3/1)
sDn,dDn	D ddd1	4 0sss									2	4(1/0)
AND.B												
data8,dadr	0 2	00ff ffff	00	yy	[EXT]						4, 6, or 8	13(2/1)+
data8,Dn	0 2	0 0ddd	00	yy							4	8(2/0)
data8,SR	0 2	3 C	00	yy							4	20(3/0)
Dn,dadr	C sss1	00ff ffff	[EXT]								2, 4, or 6	9(1/1)+
sadr,Dn	C ddd0	00ee eeee	[EXT]								2, 4, or 6	4(1/0)+
sDn,dDn	C ddd0	00ee eeee									2	4(1/0)
AND.L												
data32,dadr	0 2	10ff ffff	yyyy		zzzz		[EXT]		[EXT]		6, 8, or 10	22(3/2)+
data32,Dn	0 2	8 0ddd	yyyy		zzzz						6	16(3/0)
Dn,dadr	C sss1	10ff ffff	[EXT]								2, 4, or 6	14(1/2)+
sadr,Dn	C ddd0	10ee eeee	[EXT]								2, 4, or 6	6(1/0)+
sDn,dDn	C ddd0	10ee eeee									2	8(1/0)
AND.W												
data16,dadr	0 2	01ff ffff	yyyy		[EXT]						4, 6, or 8	13(2/1)+
data16,Dn	0 2	4 0ddd	yyyy								4	8(2/0)
data16,SR	0 2	7 C	yyyy								4	20(3/0)
Dn,dadr	C sss1	01ff ffff	[EXT]								2, 4, or 6	9(1/1)
sadr,Dn	C ddd0	01ee eeee	[EXT]								2, 4, or 6	4(1/0)

Table B-1. MC68000 Instruction Object Codes (Continued)

Instruction		Byte 1	Byte 2	Byte 3	Byte 4	Byte 5	Byte 6	Byte 7	Byte 8	Byte 9	Byte 10	Bytes	Clock Cycles
	sDn,dDn	C ddd0	4 0sss									2	4(1/0)
ASL	dadr	E 1	11ff ffff	[EXT]								2, 4, or 6	9(1/1)+
ASL.B	count,Dn	E ccc1	0 0ddd									2	6+2N(1/0)
	Dn,dDn	E rrr1	2 0ddd									2	6+2N(1/0)
ASL.L	count,Dn	E ccc1	8 0ddd									2	8+2N(1/0)
	Dn,dDn	E rrr1	A 0ddd									2	8+2N(1/0)
ASL.W	count,Dn	E ccc1	4 0ddd									2	6+2N(1/0)
	Dn,dDn	E rrr1	6 0ddd									2	6+2N(1/0)
ASR	dadr	E 0	11ff ffff	[EXT]								2, 4, or 6	9(1/1)+
ASR.B	count,Dn	E ccc0	0 0ddd									2	6+2N(1/0)
	Dn,dDn	E rrr0	2 0ddd									2	6+2N(1/0)
ASR.L	count,Dn	E ccc0	8 0ddd									2	8+2N(1/0)
	Dn,dDn	E rrr0	A 0ddd									2	8+2N(1/0)
ASR.W	count,Dn	E ccc0	4 0ddd									2	6+2N(1/0)
	Dn,dDn	E rrr0	6 0ddd									2	6+2N(1/0)
BCC	label	6 4	x 0	xxxx		[EXT]						4	10, 12(2/0)
	label	6 4	x x									4	10, 18(1/0)
BCHG	bitb,dadr	0 8	01ff ffff	00	0 0bbb	[EXT]	[EXT]	[EXT]				4, 6, or 8	13(2/1)+
	bit1,Dn	0 8	4 0ddd	00	000b bbbb							4	12(2/0)
	Dn,dadr	0 rrr1	01ff ffff	[EXT]								2, 4, or 6	9(1/1)+
	Dn,dDn	0 rrr1	4 0ddd									2	8(1/0)
BCLR	bitb,dadr	0 8	10ff ffff	00	0 0bbb	[EXT]	[EXT]	[EXT]				4, 6, or 8	13(2/1)+
	bit1,Dn	0 8	8 0ddd	00	000b bbbb							4	14(2/0)
	Dn,dadr	0 rrr1	10ff ffff	[EXT]								2, 4, or 6	9(1/1)+
	Dn,dDn	0 rrr1	8 0ddd									2	8(1/0)
BCS	label	6 5	x 0	xxxx								4	10, 12(2/0)
BEQ	label	6 7	x 0	xxxx								4	10, 18(1/0)
BGE	label	6 C	x 0	xxxx								4	10, 12(2/0)
BGT	label	6 E	x 0	xxxx								4	10, 12(2/0)
BHI	label	6 E	x 0	xxxx								4	10, 12(2/0)
BLE	label	6 2	x 0	xxxx								4	10, 8(1/0)
BLS	label	6 F	x 0	xxxx								4	10, 12(2/0)
BLT	label	6 3	x 0	xxxx								4	10, 8(1/0)
BMI	label	6 D	x 0	xxxx								4	10, 12(2/0)
BNE	label	6 D	x 0	xxxx								4	10, 12(2/0)
BPL	label	6 B	x 0	xxxx								4	10, 8(1/0)
	label	6 6	x 0	xxxx								4	10, 12(2/0)
	label	6 A	x 0	xxxx								4	10, 12(2/0)
BRA	label	6 0	x 0	xxxx								4	10, 8(1/0)
	label	6 0	x x									2	10, 8(1/0)
BSET	bitb,dadr	0 8	11ff ffff	00	0 0bbb	[EXT]	[EXT]	[EXT]				4, 6, or 8	13(2/1)+
	bit1,Dn	0 8	C 0ddd	00	000b bbbb							4	12(2/0)
	Dn,dadr	0 rrr1	11ff ffff	[EXT]								2, 4, or 6	9(1/1)+
	Dn,dDn	0 rrr1	C 0ddd									2	8(1/0)

Table B-1. MC68000 Instruction Object Codes (Continued)

Instruction		Byte 1	Byte 2	Byte 3	Byte 4	Byte 5	Byte 6	Byte 7	Byte 8	Byte 9	Byte 10	Bytes	Clock Cycles
BSR	label	6 1	0 0	x x x x								4	10, 12(2/0)
	label	6 1	x x									2	10, 8(1/0)
BTST	bitb,dadr	0 8	00ff ffff	0 0	0 0bbb bbbb	[EXT]						4, 6, or 8	8(2/0)+
	bit,Dn	0 8	0 0ddd	0 0	000bbbbb							4	10(2/0)
	Dn,dadr	0 rrr1	00ff ffff	[EXT]								2, 4, or 6	4(1/0)
	Dn,dDn	0 rrr1	0 0ddd									2	6(1/0)
BVC	label	6 8	0 0	x x x x								4	10, 12(2/0)
	label	6 8	x x									2	10, 8(1/0)
BVS	label	6 9	0 0	x x x x								4	10, 12(2/0)
	label	6 9	x x									2	10, 8(1/0)
CHK	data16,Dn	4 ddd1	B C	y y y y								4	49(6/3), 12(2/0)
	Dn,dDn	4 ddd1	8 0rrr									2	45(5/3), 8(1/0)
	sadr,Dn	4 ddd1	10ee eeee	[EXT]								2, 4, or 6	45(5/3)+, 8(1/0)
CLR.B	dadr	4 2	00ff ffff	[EXT]								2, 4, or 6	9(1/1)+
	Dn	4 2	0 0ddd									2	4(1/0)
CLR.L	dadr	4 2	10ff ffff	[EXT]								2, 4, or 6	14(1/2)+
	Dn	4 2	8 0ddd									2	6(1/0)
CLR.W	dadr	4 2	01ff ffff	[EXT]								2, 4, or 6	9(1/1)
	Dn	4 2	4 0ddd									2	4(1/0)
CMP.B	data8,dadr	0 C	00ff ffff	0 0	x x	[EXT]						4, 6, or 8	8(2/0)
	data8,Dn	0 C	0 0ddd	0 0	x x							4	8(2/0)
	sadr,Dn	B ddd0	00ee eeee	[EXT]								2, 4, or 6	4(1/0)+
	sDn,dDn	B ddd0	0 0sss									2	4(1/0)
CMP.L	data32,An	B ddd1	F C	z z z z	z z z z	[EXT]						6	14(3/0)
	data32,dadr	0 C	10ff ffff	y y y y	z z z z	[EXT]						6, 8, or 10	12(3/0)+
	data32,Dn	0 C	8 0ddd	y y y y	z z z z							6	14(3/0)
	rs,An	B ddd1	C 0sss									2	6(1/0)
	rs,Dn	B ddd0	8 0sss									2	6(1/0)
	sadr,An	B ddd1	11ee eeee	[EXT]								2, 4, or 6	6(1/0)+
	sadr,Dn	B ddd0	10ee eeee	[EXT]								2, 4, or 6	6(1/0)+
CMP.W	data16,An	B ddd0	F C	y y y y								4	8(2/0)
	data16,dadr	0 C	01ff ffff	y y y y	[EXT]							4, 6, or 8	8(2/0)
	data16,Dn	0 C	4 0ddd	y y y y								4	8(2/0)
	rs,An	B ddd0	C 0sss									2	6(1/0)
	rs,Dn	B ddd0	4 0sss									2	4(1/0)
	sadr,An	B ddd0	11ee eeee	[EXT]								2, 4, or 6	6(1/0)+
	sadr,Dn	B ddd0	01ee eeee	[EXT]								2, 4, or 6	4(1/0)+
CMPM.B	(sAn)+,(dAn)+	B ddd1	0 1sss									2	12(3/0)
CMPM.L	(sAn)+,(dAn)+	B ddd1	8 1sss									2	20(5/0)
CMPM.W	(sAn)+,(dAn)+	B ddd1	4 1sss									2	12(3/0)
DBCC	Dn,label	5 4	C 1rrr	x x x x								4	12(2/0), 10(2/0), 14(3/0)
DBCS	Dn,label	5 5	C 1rrr	x x x x								4	12(2/0), 10(2/0), 14(3/0)
DBEQ	Dn,label	5 7	C 1rrr	x x x x								4	12(2/0), 10(2/0), 14(3/0)
DBF	Dn,label	5 1	C 1rrr	x x x x								4	12(2/0), 10(2/0), 14(3/0)
DBGE	Dn,label	5 C	C 1rrr	x x x x								4	12(2/0), 10(2/0), 14(3/0)
DBGT	Dn,label	5 E	C 1rrr	x x x x								4	12(2/0), 10(2/0), 14(3/0)
DBHI	Dn,label	5 2	C 1rrr	x x x x								4	12(2/0), 10(2/0), 14(3/0)
DBLE	Dn,label	5 F	C 1rrr	x x x x								4	12(2/0), 10(2/0), 14(3/0)
DBLS	Dn,label	5 3	C 1rrr	x x x x								4	12(2/0), 10(2/0), 14(3/0)
DBLT	Dn,label	5 D	C 1rrr	x x x x								4	12(2/0), 10(2/0), 14(3/0)
DBMI	Dn,label	5 B	C 1rrr	x x x x								4	12(2/0), 10(2/0), 14(3/0)
DBNE	Dn,label	5 6	C 1rrr	x x x x								4	12(2/0), 10(2/0), 14(3/0)
DBPL	Dn,label	5 A	C 1rrr	x x x x								4	12(2/0), 10(2/0), 14(3/0)

Table B-1. MC68000 Instruction Object Codes (Continued)

Instruction		Byte 1	Byte 2	Byte 3	Byte 4	Byte 5	Byte 6	Byte 7	Byte 8	Byte 9	Byte 10	Bytes	Clock Cycles
DBRA	Dn,label	(same as DBF)										4	12(2/0),10(2/0),14(3/0)
DBT	Dn,label	5 0	C 1rrr	xxxx								4	12(2/0),10(2/0),14(3/0)
DVC	Dn,label	5 8	C 1rrr	xxxx								4	12(2/0),10(2/0),14(3/0)
DVS	Dn,label	5 9	C 1rrr	xxxx								4	12(2/0),10(2/0),14(3/0)
DIVS	data16,Dn	8 ddd1	F C	yyyy								4	<162(2/0)
	sadr,Dn	8 ddd1	1ee eeee	[EXT]		[EXT]						2, 4, or 6	<158(1/0)+
	sDn,dDn	8 ddd1	C 0sss									2	<158(1/0)
DIVU	data16,Dn	8 ddd0	F C	yyyy								4	<148(2/0)
	sadr,Dn	8 ddd0	1ee eeee	[EXT]		[EXT]						2, 4, or 6	<140(1/0)+
	sDn,dDn	8 ddd0	C 0sss									2	<140(1/0)
EOR.B	data8,dadr	0 A	00ff ffff	00	yy	[EXT]		[EXT]				4, 6, or 8	13(2/1)+
	data8.Dn	0 A	0 0ddd	00	yy							4	8(2/0)
	data8.SR	0 A	3 C	00	yy							4	20(3/0)
	Dn,dadr	B sss1	00ff ffff	[EXT]		[EXT]						2, 4, or 6	9(1/1)+
	sDn,dDn	B sss1	0 0ddd									2	4(1/0)
EOR.L	data32,dadr	0 A	10ff ffff	yyyy		zzzz		[EXT]		[EXT]		6, 8, or 10	22(3/2)+
	data32,Dn	0 A	8 0ddd	yyyy		zzzz						6	16(3/0)
	Dn,dadr	B sss1	10ff ffff	[EXT]		[EXT]		[EXT]				2, 4, or 6	14(1/2)+
	sDn,dDn	B sss1	8 0ddd									2	8(1/0)
EOR.W	data16,dadr	0 A	01ff ffff	yyyy		[EXT]		[EXT]				4, 6, or 8	13(2/1)+
	data16,Dn	0 A	4 0ddd	yyyy								4	8(2/0)
	data16,Sr	0 A	7 C	yyyy								4	20(3/0)
	Dn,dadr	B sss1	01ff ffff	[EXT]		[EXT]						2, 4, or 6	9(1/1)+
	sDn,dDn	B sss1	4 0ddd									2	4(1/0)
EXG	An,An	(same as An,Dn)										2	6(1/0)
	Dn,An	C sss1	8 1ddd									2	6(1/0)
	Dn,Dn	C sss1	4 0ddd									2	6(1/0)
EXT.L	Dn	4 8	C 0ddd									2	4(1/0)
EXT.W	Dn	4 8	8 0ddd									2	4(1/0)
JMP	jadr	4 E	11jjjjjj	[EXT]		[EXT]						2, 4, or 6	4(1/0)+
JSR	jadr	4 E	10jjjjjj	[EXT]		[EXT]						2, 4, or 6	14(1/2)+
LEA	jadr,An	4 ddd1	11ff ffff	[EXT]		[EXT]						2, 4, or 6	2(0/0)+
LINK	An,d16	4 E	5 0rrr	yyyy								4	18(2/2)
LSL	dadr	E 3	11ff ffff	[EXT]		[EXT]						2, 4, or 6	9(1/1)+
LSL.B	count,Dn	E ccc1	0 1ddd									2	6 + 2N(1/0)
	Dn,dDn	E rrr1	2 1ddd									2	6 + 2N(1/0)
LSL.L	count,Dn	E ccc1	8 1ddd									2	8 + 2N(1/0)
	Dn,dDn	E rrr1	A 1ddd									2	8 + 2N(1/0)
LSL.W	count,Dn	E ccc1	4 1ddd									2	6 + 2N(1/0)
	Dn,dDn	E rrr1	6 1ddd									2	6 + 2N(1/0)
LSR	dadr	E 2	11ff ffff	[EXT]		[EXT]						2, 4, or 6	9(1/1)+
LSR.B	count,Dn	E ccc0	0 1ddd									2	6 + 2N(1/0)
	Dn,dDn	E rrr0	2 1ddd									2	6 + 2N(1/0)
LSR.L	count,Dn	E ccc0	8 1ddd									2	8 + 2N(1/0)
	Dn,dDn	E rrr0	A 1ddd									2	8 + 2N(1/0)
LSR.W	count,Dn	E ccc0	4 1ddd									2	6 + 2N(1/0)
	Dn,dDn	E rrr0	6 1ddd									2	6 + 2N(1/0)
MOVE	An,USP	4 E	6 0rrr									2	4(1/0)
	data8,CCR	4 4	F C	00	yy							4	16(3/0)
	data16,SR	4 6	F C	yyyy								4	16(3/0)
	Dn,CCR	4 4	C 0sss									2	12(2/0)
	Dn,SR	4 6	C 0sss									2	12(2/0)

Table B-1. MC68000 Instruction Object Codes (Continued)

Instruction		Byte 1	Byte 2	Byte 3	Byte 4	Byte 5	Byte 6	Byte 7	Byte 8	Byte 9	Byte 10	Bytes	Clock Cycles
MOVE.8	sadr,CCR	44	11eeeeee	[EXT]		[EXT]						2, 4, or 6	12(2/0)+
	sadr,SR	46	11eeeeee	[EXT]		[EXT]						2, 4, or 6	12(2/0)+
	SR,dadr	40	11ffffff	[EXT]		[EXT]						2, 4, or 6	9(1/1)+
	SR,Dn	40	C 0ddd									2	6(1/0)
	USP,An	4E	6 1sss									2	4(1/0)
	data8,Dn	1 ddd0	3 C		yy							4	8(2/0)
	data8,dadr	1 ggg	ggg11C		yy	[EXT]		[EXT]				4, 6, or 8	9(1/1)+
	Dn,dadr	1 ggg	ggg000sss	[EXT]		[EXT]						2, 4, or 6	5(0/1)+
	sDn,dDn	1 ddd0	0 0sss									2	4(1/0)
MOVE.L	sadr,dadr	2 ggg	ggg000Osss	[EXTs]		[EXTs]		[EXTd]		[EXTd]		2, 4, 6, 8 or 10	5(1/1)+
	An,dadr	2 ggg	ggg001sss	[EXT]		[EXT]						2, 4, or 6	4(1/0)
	data32,An	2 ddd0	7 C	yyyy		yyyy						6	10(0/2)+
	data32,dadr	2 ggg	ggg11C	yyyy		yyyy		zzzz		zzzz		6	12(3/0)
	data32,Dn	2 ddd0	3 C	yyyy		yyyy						6, 8, or 10	12(3/0)
	Dn,dadr	2 ggg	ggg000 0sss	[EXT]		[EXT]						6	10(0/2)+
	rs,An	2 ddd0	4 tsss									2, 4, or 6	4(1/0)
	rs,Dn	2 ddd0	0 tsss									2	4(1/0)
MOVE.W	sadr,An	3 ddd0	01eeeeee	[EXT]		[EXT]						2	8(2/0)+
	sadr,dadr	3 ggg	ggg eeeeee	[EXTs]		[EXTs]		[EXTd]		[EXTd]		2, 4, 6, 8, or 10	8(2/0)+
	An,dadr	3 ggg	ggg000eeeeee	[EXT]		[EXT]						2, 4, or 6	14(1/2)+
	data16,An	3 ddd0	7 C	yyyy		[EXT]						2, 4, or 6	4(1/0)+
	data16,dadr	3 ggg	ggg001sss	yyyy		[EXT]						4, 6, or 8	5(0/1)+
	data16,Dn	3 ddd0	ggg11C	yyyy		[EXT]						2, 4, or 6	8(2/0)
	Dn,dadr	3 ggg	3 C	[EXT]		[EXT]						2, 4, or 6	9(1/1)+
	rs,An	3 ddd0	ggg000 0sss									2	8(2/0)
	rs,Dn	3 ddd0	4 tsss									2	5(0/1)+
	sadr,An	3 ddd0	0 tsss	[EXT]		[EXT]						2, 4, or 6	4(1/0)
	sadr,dadr	3 ggg	01eeeeee	[EXTs]		[EXTs]		[EXTd]				2	4(1/0)
	sadr,Dn	3 ggg	ggg000eeeeee	[EXT]		[EXT]						2	4(1/0)+
MOVEM.L	(An)+,reg-list	4C	E 0sss	mmmm		[EXT]						4	8 + 8n(2 + 2n/0)+
	jadr,reg-list	4C	1jjjjjj	kkkk		[EXT]		[EXT]				4, 6, or 8	8 + 8n(2 + 2n/0)+
	reg-list,-(An)	48	E 0ddd	mmmm		[EXT]						4	4 + 10n(1/n)
	reg-list,madr	48	11hhhhhh	mmmm		[EXT]		[EXT]				4, 6, or 8	4 + 10n(1/n)+
MOVEM.W	(An)+,reg-list	4C	A 0sss	mmmm		[EXT]						4	8 + 4n(2 + n/0)
	jadr,reg-list	4C	10jjjjjj	kkkk		[EXT]		[EXT]				4, 6, or 8	8 + 4n(2 + n/0)+
	reg-list,-(An)	48	A 0ddd	mmmm		[EXT]						4	4 + 5n1(1/n)
	reg-list,madr	48	10hhhhhh	mmmm		[EXT]		[EXT]				4, 6, or 8	4 + 5n1(1/n)+
MOVEP.L	d16(An),Dn	0 ddd1	4 1sss	xxxx		[EXT]		[EXT]				4	24(6/0)
	Dn,d16(An)	0 sss1	C 0 1ddd	xxxx		[EXT]		[EXT]				4	24(2/4)
MOVEP.W	d16(An),Dn	0 ddd1	C 0 1sss	xxxx		[EXT]		[EXT]				4	16(4/0)
	Dn,d16(An)	0 sss1	8 1ddd	xxxx		[EXT]		[EXT]				4	16(2/2)
MOVEQ	data8,Dn	7 ddd0	F C	yyyy								4	4(1/0)
MULS	data16,Dn	C ddd1	11eeeeee	yyyy		[EXT]						2, 4, or 6	<74(2/0)
	sDn,Dn	C ddd1	F C	[EXT]								2	<70(1/0)+
MULU	data16,Dn	C ddd0	1eeeeee	yyyy		[EXT]						2, 4, or 6	<74(2/0)
	sDn,Dn	C ddd0	C 0sss	[EXT]								2	<70(1/0)+
NBCD	dadr	48	0 0ddd	[EXT]		[EXT]						2, 4, or 6	8(1/1)+
	Dn	48	00ff ffff									2	6(1/0)
NEG.B	dadr	44	00ff ffff	[EXT]		[EXT]						2, 4, or 6	9(1/1)+

Table B-1. MC68000 Instruction Object Codes (Continued)

Instruction		Byte 1	Byte 2	Byte 3	Byte 4	Byte 5	Byte 6	Byte 7	Byte 8	Byte 9	Byte 10	Bytes	Clock Cycles
NEG.L	Dn	4	0 0ddd									2	4(1/0)
	dadr	4	10ff ffff	[EXT]								2, 4, or 6	14(1/2)+
NEG.W	Dn	4	8 0ddd									2	6(1/0)
	dadr	4	01ff ffff	[EXT]								2, 4, or 6	9(1/1)
NEGX.B	Dn	4	00ff ffff									2	4(1/0)
	dadr	0	0 0ddd	[EXT]								2, 4, or 6	9(1/1)+
NEGX.L	Dn	0	10ff ffff									2	4(1/0)
	dadr	0	8 0ddd	[EXT]								2, 4, or 6	14(1/2)+
NEGX.W	Dn	0	01ff ffff									2	6(1/0)
	dadr	0	4 0ddd	[EXT]								2, 4, or 6	9(1/1)+
NOP		4	7 1									2	4(1/0)
NOT.B	dadr	E	00ff ffff	[EXT]								2, 4, or 6	9(1/1)+
	Dn	4	0 0ddd									2	4(1/0)
NOT.L	dadr	6	10ff ffff	[EXT]								2, 4, or 6	14(1/2)+
	Dn	4	8 0ddd									2	6(1/0)
NOT.W	dadr	6	01ff ffff	[EXT]								2, 4, or 6	9(1/1)+
OR.B	data8,dadr	4	4 0ddd	00	yy	[EXT]						4, 6, or 8	13(2/1)+
	data8,Dn	6	00ff ffff	00	yy							4	8(2/0)
	data8,SR	4	0 0ddd	00	yy							4	20(3/0)
	Dn,dadr	0	00eeeeee	[EXT]								2, 4, or 6	9(1/1)+
	sadr,Dn	0	3 C	[EXT]								2, 4, or 6	4(1/0)+
	sDn,dDn	0	0 0sss									2	4(1/0)
OR.L	data32,dadr	8	00ff ffff	yyyy		zzzz		[EXT]				6, 8, or 10	22(3/2)+
	data32,Dn	8	0 0ddd	yyyy		zzzz						6	16(3/0)
	Dn,dadr	0	10ff ffff	[EXT]		[EXT]						2, 4, or 6	14(1/2)+
	sadr,Dn	0	10eeeeee	[EXT]		[EXT]						2, 4, or 6	6(1/0)+
	sDn,dDn	8	8 0sss									2	8(1/0)
OR.W	data16,dadr	8	01ff ffff	yyyy		[EXT]		[EXT]				4, 6, or 8	13(2/1)+
	data16,Dn	0	0 0ddd	yyyy								4	8(2/0)
	data16,SR	0	01eeeeee	yyyy								4	20(3/0)
	Dn,dadr	0	7 C	[EXT]		[EXT]						2, 4, or 6	9(1/1)+
	sadr,Dn	8	10ff ffff	[EXT]		[EXT]		[EXT]				2, 4, or 6	4(1/0)
	sDn,dDn	8	4 0sss									2	4(1/0)
PEA	jadr	4	01ji jjjj	[EXT]		[EXT]		[EXT]				2, 4, or 6	10(1/2)+
RESET		4	7 0									2	132(1/0)
ROL	dadr	E	11ff ffff	[EXT]		[EXT]						2, 4, or 6	9(1/1)+
ROLB	count,Dn	E ccc1	1 1ddd									2	6+2N(1/0)
	Dn,dDn	E rrr1	3 1ddd									2	8+2N(1/0)
ROLL	count,Dn	E ccc1	9 1ddd									2	8+2N(1/0)
	Dn,dDn	E rrr1	B 1ddd									2	6+2N(1/0)
ROLW	count,Dn	E ccc1	5 1ddd									2	6+2N(1/0)
	Dn,dDn	E rrr1	7 1ddd									2	6+2N(1/0)
ROR	dadr	E	11ff ffff	[EXT]								2, 4, or 6	9(1/1)+
RORB	count,Dn	E ccc0	1 1ddd									2	6+2N(1/0)
	Dn,dDn	E rrr0	3 1ddd									2	8+2N(1/0)
RORL	count,Dn	E ccc0	9 1ddd									2	8+2N(1/0)
	Dn,dDn	E rrr0	B 1ddd									2	6+2N(1/0)
RORW	count,Dn	E ccc0	5 1ddd									2	6+2N(1/0)
	Dn,dDn	E rrr0	7 1ddd									2	6+2N(1/0)
ROXL	dadr	5	11ff ffff	[EXT]								2, 4, or 6	9(1/1)+
ROXLB	count,Dn	E ccc1	1 0ddd									2	6+2N(1/0)

Table B-1. MC68000 Instruction Object Codes (Continued)

Instruction	Byte 1	Byte 2	Byte 3	Byte 4	Byte 5	Byte 6	Byte 7	Byte 8	Byte 9	Byte 10	Bytes	Clock Cycles
ROXL.L Dn,dDn	E rrr1	B Oddd									2	6 + 2N(1/0)
ROXL.L count,Dn	E ccc1	9 Oddd									2	8 + 2N(1/0)
ROXL.W Dn,dDn	E rrr1	7 Oddd									2	8 + 2N(1/0)
ROXL.W count,Dn	E ccc1	5 Oddd									2	6 + 2N(1/0)
ROXR dadr	E 4	11ff ffff	[EXT]								2, 4, or 6	9(1/1)+
ROXR.B count,Dn	E ccc0	1 Oddd									2	6 + 2N(1/0)
ROXR.B Dn,dDn	E rrr0	3 Oddd									2	6 + 2N(1/0)
ROXR.L count,Dn	E ccc0	9 Oddd									2	8 + 2N(1/0)
ROXR.L Dn,dDn	E rrr0	B Oddd									2	8 + 2N(1/0)
ROXR.W count,Dn	E ccc0	5 Oddd									2	6 + 2N(1/0)
ROXR.W Dn,dDn	E rrr0	7 Oddd									2	6 + 2N(1/0)
RTE	4 E	7 3									2	20(5/0)
RTR	4 E	7 7									2	20(5/0)
RTS	4 E	7 5									2	16(4/0)
SBCD -(sAn),-(dAn)	8 ddd1	0 1sss									2	18(3/1)
SBCD sDn,dDn	8 ddd1	0 Osss									2	6(1/0)
SCC dadr	5 4	11ff ffff	[EXT]								2, 4, or 6	9(1/1)+
SCC Dn	5 4	C Oddd									2	6, 4(1/0)
SCS dadr	5 5	11ff ffff	[EXT]								2, 4, or 6	9(1/1)+
SCS Dn	5 5	C Oddd									2	6, 4(1/0)
SEQ dadr	5 7	11ff ffff	[EXT]								2, 4, or 6	9(1/1)+
SEQ Dn	5 7	C Oddd									2	6, 4(1/0)
SF dadr	5 1	11ff ffff	[EXT]								2, 4, or 6	9(1/1)+
SF Dn	5 1	C Oddd									2	6, 4(1/0)
SGE dadr	5 C	11ff ffff	[EXT]								2, 4, or 6	9(1/1)+
SGE Dn	5 C	C Oddd									2	6, 4(1/0)
SGT dadr	5 E	11ff ffff	[EXT]								2, 4, or 6	9(1/1)+
SGT Dn	5 E	C Oddd									2	6, 4(1/0)
SHI dadr	5 2	11ff ffff	[EXT]								2, 4, or 6	9(1/1)+
SHI Dn	5 2	C Oddd									2	6, 4(1/0)
SLE dadr	5 F	11ff ffff	[EXT]								2, 4, or 6	9(1/1)+
SLE Dn	5 F	C Oddd									2	6, 4(1/0)
SLS dadr	5 3	11ff ffff	[EXT]								2, 4, or 6	9(1/1)+
SLS Dn	5 3	C Oddd									2	6, 4(1/0)
SLT dadr	5 D	11ff ffff	[EXT]								2, 4, or 6	9(1/1)+
SLT Dn	5 D	C Oddd									2	6, 4(1/0)
SMI dadr	5 B	11ff ffff	[EXT]								2, 4, or 6	9(1/1)+
SMI Dn	5 B	C Oddd									2	6, 4(1/0)
SNE dadr	5 6	11ff ffff	[EXT]								2, 4, or 6	9(1/1)+
SNE Dn	5 6	C Oddd									2	6, 4(1/0)
SPL dadr	5 A	11ff ffff	[EXT]								2, 4, or 6	9(1/1)+
SPL Dn	5 A	C Oddd									2	6, 4(1/0)
ST dadr	5 0	11ff ffff	[EXT]								2, 4, or 6	9(1/1)+
ST Dn	5 0	C Oddd									2	6, 4(1/0)
STOP data16	4 E	7 2	yyyy								4	8(2/0)
SUB.B data8,dadr	0 4	OOff ffff	00	yy	[EXT]						4, 6, or 8	13(2/1)+
SUB.B data8,Dn	0 4	O Oddd	00	yy							4	8(2/0)
SUB.B Dn,dadr	9 ddd1	OOff ffff	[EXT]								2, 4, or 6	9(1/1)+
SUB.B sadr,Dn	9 ddd0	OOee eeee	[EXT]								2, 4, or 6	4(1/0)+
SUB.B sDn,dDn	9 ddd0	0 Osss									2	4(1/0)
SUB.L data32,An	9 ddd1	F C	yyyy		zzzz						6	16(3/0)
SUB.L data32,dadr	0 4	10ff ffff	yyyy		zzzz		[EXT]				6, 8, or 10	22(3/2)+

Table B-1. MC68000 Instruction Object Code Tables (Continued)

Instruction	Byte 1	Byte 2	Byte 3	Byte 4	Byte 5	Byte 6	Byte 7	Byte 8	Byte 9	Byte 10	Bytes	Clock Cycles
data32,Dn	0 4 .	8 0ddd	yyyy		zzzz						6	16(3/0)
Dn,dadr	9 sss1	10ff ffff	[EXT]								2, 4, or 6	14(1/2)+
rs,An	9 ddd0	C tss									2	8(1/0)
rs,Dn	9 ddd0	8 tsss									2	8(1/0)
sadr,An	9 ddd1	11eeeeee	[EXT]								2, 4, or 6	6(1/0)+
sadr,Dn	9 ddd0	10eeeeee	[EXT]								2, 4, or 6	6(1/0)+
SUB.W data16,An	9 ddd0	F C	yyyy								4	8(2/0)
data16,dadr	0 4	01ff ffff	yyyy		[EXT]						4, 6, or 8	13(2/1)+
data16,Dn	0 4	4 0ddd	yyyy								4	8(2/0)
Dn,dadr	9 sss1	01ff ffff	[EXT]								2, 4, or 6	9(1/1)+
rs,An	9 ddd0	C tss									2	8(1/0)
rs,Dn	9 ddd0	0 tss									2	4(1/0)
sadr,An	9 ddd0	11eeeeee	[EXT]								2, 4, or 6	8(1/0)+
sadr,Dn	9 ddd0	01eeeeee	[EXT]								2, 4, or 6	4(1/0)+
SUBQ.B data3,dadr	5 bbb1	00ff ffff	[EXT]								2, 4, or 6	9(1/1)+
data3,Dn	5 bbb1	0 0ddd									2	4(1/0)
SUBQ.L data3,dadr	5 bbb1	10ff ffff	[EXT]								2, 4, or 6	8(1/0)+
data3,Dn	5 bbb1	8 0ddd									2	8(1/0)
SUBQ.W data3,An	5 bbb1	4 1ddd									2	8(1/0)
data3,dadr	5 bbb1	01ff ffff	[EXT]								2, 4, or 6	9(1/1)+
data3,Dn	5 bbb1	4 0ddd									2	4(1/0)
SUBX.B -(sAn),-(dAn)	9 ddd1	0 1sss									2	19(3/1)
sDn,dDn	9 ddd1	0 0sss									2	4(1/0)
SUBX.L -(sAn),-(dAn)	9 ddd1	8 1sss									2	32(5/2)
sDn,dDn	9 ddd1	8 0sss									2	8(1/0)
SUBX.W -(sAn),-(dAn)	9 ddd1	4 1sss									2	19(3/1)
sDn,dDn	9 ddd1	4 0sss									2	4(1/0)
SVC dadr	5 8	11ff ffff	[EXT]								2, 4, or 6	9(1/1)+
Dn	5 8	C 0ddd									2	6, 4(1/0)
SVS dadr	5 9	11ff ffff	[EXT]								2, 4, or 6	9(1/1)+
Dn	5 9	C 0ddd									2	6, 4(1/0)
SWAP Dn	4 8	4 0rrr									2	4(1/0)
TAS dadr	4 A	11ff ffff	[EXT]								2, 4, or 6	11(1/1)+
Dn	4 A	C 0rrr									2	4(1/0)
TRAP vector	4 E	4 0vvv									2	36(4/3)
TRAPV	4 E	7 6									2	37(5/3), 4(1/0)
TST.B dadr	4 A	00ff ffff	[EXT]								2, 4, or 6	4(1/0)+
Dn	4 A	0 0rrr									2	4(1/0)
TST.L dadr	4 A	10ff ffff	[EXT]								2, 4, or 6	4(1/0)+
Dn	4 A	8 0rrr									2	4(1/0)
TST.W dadr	4 A	01ff ffff	[EXT]								2, 4, or 6	4(1/0)+
Dn	4 A	4 0rrr									2	4(1/0)
UNLK An	4 E	5 1rrr									2	12(3/0)

Table B-2. MC68000 Object Codes in Numerical Order

Instruction		Byte 1	Byte 2	Byte 3	Byte 4	Byte 5	Byte 6	Byte 7	Byte 8	Byte 9	Byte 10
OR.B	data8,Dn	00	0 0ddd	00	yy						
OR.B	data8,dadr	00	00ff ffff	00	yy	[EXT]		[EXT]			
OR.B	data8,SR	00	3 C	00	yy						
OR.W	data16,Dn	00	4 0ddd	yyyy							
OR.W	data16,dadr	00	01ff ffff	yyyy		[EXT]		[EXT]			
OR.W	data16,SR	00	7 C	yyyy							
OR.L	data32,Dn	00	8 0ddd	yyyy		zzzz					
OR.L	data32,dadr	00	10ff ffff	yyyy		zzzz		[EXT]		[EXT]	
BTST	Dn,dDn	0rrr1	0 0ddd								
MOVEP.W	d16(An),Dn	0ddd1	0 1sss								
BTST	Dn,dadr	0rrr1	00ff ffff	[EXT]		[EXT]					
BCHG	Dn,dDn	0rrr1	A 0ddd								
MOVEP.L	d16(An),Dn	0ddd1	A 1sss	xxxx							
BCHG	Dn,dadr	0rrr1	01ff ffff	[EXT]		[EXT]					
BCLR	Dn,dDn	0rrr1	8 0ddd								
MOVEP.W	Dn,d16(An)	0sss1	8 1ddd	xxxx							
BCLR	Dn,dadr	0rrr1	10ff ffff	[EXT]		[EXT]					
BSET	Dn,dDn	0rrr1	C 0ddd								
MOVEP.L	Dn,d16(An)	0sss1	C 1ddd	xxxx							
BSET	Dn,dadr	0rrr1	11ff ffff	[EXT]		[EXT]					
AND.B	data8,Dn	02	0 0ddd	00	yy						
AND.B	data8,dadr	02	00ff ffff	00	yy	[EXT]		[EXT]			
AND.B	data8,SR	02	3 C	00	yy						
AND.W	data16,Dn	02	4 0ddd	yyyy							
AND.W	data16,dadr	02	01ff ffff	yyyy		[EXT]		[EXT]			
AND.W	data16,SR	02	7 C	yyyy							
AND.L	data32,Dn	02	8 0ddd	yyyy		zzzz					
AND.L	data32,dadr	02	10ff ffff	yyyy		zzzz		[EXT]		[EXT]	
SUB.B	data8,Dn	04	0 0ddd	00	yy						
SUB.B	data8,dadr	04	00ff ffff	00	yy	[EXT]		[EXT]			
SUB.W	data16,Dn	04	4 0ddd	yyyy							
SUB.W	data16,dadr	04	01ff ffff	yyyy		[EXT]		[EXT]			
SUB.L	data32,Dn	04	8 0ddd	yyyy		zzzz					
SUB.L	data32,dadr	04	10ff ffff	yyyy		zzzz		[EXT]		[EXT]	
ADD.B	data8,Dn	06	0 0ddd	00	yy						
ADD.B	data8,dadr	06	00ff ffff	00	yy	[EXT]		[EXT]			
ADD.W	data16,Dn	06	4 0ddd	yyyy							
ADD.W	data16,dadr	06	01ff ffff	yyyy		[EXT]		[EXT]			
ADD.L	data32,Dn	06	8 0ddd	yyyy		zzzz					
ADD.L	data32,dadr	06	10ff ffff	yyyy		zzzz		[EXT]		[EXT]	
BTST	bitl,Dn	08	0 0ddd	00	000b bbbb						
BTST	bitb,dadr	08	00ff ffff	00	0 0bbb	[EXT]		[EXT]			
BCHG	bitl,Dn	08	4 0ddd	00	000b bbbb						
BCHG	bitb,dadr	08	01ff ffff	00	0 0bbb	[EXT]		[EXT]			
BCLR	bitl,Dn	08	8 0ddd	00	000b bbbb						
BCLR	bitb,dadr	08	10ff ffff	00	0 0bbb	[EXT]		[EXT]			
BSET	bitl,Dn	08	C 0ddd	00	000b bbbb						
BSET	bitb,dadr	08	11ff ffff	00	0.0bbb	[EXT]		[EXT]			
EOR.B	data8,Dn	0A	0 0ddd	00	yy						
EOR.B	data8,dadr	0A	00ff ffff	00	yy	[EXT]		[EXT]			
EOR.B	data8,SR	0A	3 C		yy						
EOR.W	data16,Dn	0A	4 0ddd	yyyy							
EOR.W	data16,dadr	0A	01ff ffff	yyyy		[EXT]		[EXT]			
EOR.W	data16,SR	0A	7 C	yyyy							
EOR.L	data32,Dn	0A	8 0ddd	yyyy		zzzz					
EOR.L	data32,dadr	0A	10ff ffff	yyyy		zzzz		[EXT]		[EXT]	
CMP.B	data8,Dn	0C	0 0ddd	00	yy						
CMP.B	data8,dadr	0C	00ff ffff	00	yy	[EXT]		[EXT]			
CMP.W	data16,Dn	0C	4 0ddd	yyyy							
CMP.W	data16,dadr	0C	01ff ffff	yyyy		[EXT]		[EXT]			
CMP.L	data32,Dn	0C	8 0ddd	yyyy		zzzz					
CMP.L	data32,dadr	0C	10ff ffff	yyyy		zzzz		[EXT]		[EXT]	
MOVE.B	sDn,dDn	1 ddd0	0 0sss								
MOVE.B	sadr,Dn	1 ddd0	00ee eeee	[EXT]		[EXT]					
MOVE.B	data8,Dn	1 ddd0	3 C	00	yy						
MOVE.B	Dn,dadr	1 gggg	gg00 0sss	[EXT]		[EXT]					
MOVE.B	sadr,dadr	1 gggg	ggee eeee	[EXTs]		[EXTs]		[EXTd]		[EXTd]	
MOVE.B	data8,dadr	1 gggg	gg11 C	00	yy	[EXT]		[EXT]			
MOVE.L	rs,Dn	2 ddd0	0000 tsss								
MOVE.L	sadr,Dn	2 ddd0	00ee eeee	[EXT]		[EXT]					
MOVE.L	data32,Dn	2 ddd0	3 C	yyyy		zzzz					
MOVE.L	rs,An	2 ddd0	0100 tsss								
MOVE.L	sadr,An	2 ddd0	01ee eeee	[EXT]		[EXT]					

Table B-2. MC68000 Object Codes in Numerical Order (Continued)

Instruction		Byte 1	Byte 2	Byte 3	Byte 4	Byte 5	Byte 6	Byte 7	Byte 8	Byte 9	Byte 10
MOVE.L	data32,An	2ddd0	7 C	yyyy		zzzz					
MOVE.L	rs,dadr	2gggg	gg00tsss	[EXT]		[EXT]					
MOVE.L	sadr,dadr	2gggg	ggee eeee	[EXT$_s$]		[EXT$_s$]		[EXT$_d$]		[EXT$_d$]	
MOVE.L	data32,dadr	2gggg	gg11C	yyyy		zzzz		[EXT]		[EXT]	
MOVE.W	rs,Dn	3ddd0	0 tsss								
MOVE.W	sadr,Dn	3ddd0	00ee eeee	[EXT]		[EXT]					
MOVE.W	data16,Dn	3ddd0	3 C	yyyy							
MOVE.W	rs,An	3ddd0	4 tsss								
MOVE.W	sadr,An	3ddd0	01ee eeee	[EXT]		[EXT]					
MOVE.W	data16,An	3ddd0	7 C	yyyy							
MOVE.W	rs,dadr	3gggg	gg00tsss	[EXT]		[EXT]					
MOVE.W	sadr,dadr	3gggg	ggee eeee	[EXT$_s$]		[EXT$_s$]		[EXT$_d$]		[EXT$_d$]	
MOVE.W	data16,dadr	3gggg	gg11C	yyyy		[EXT]		[EXT]			
NEGX.B	Dn	40	0 0ddd								
NEGX.B	dadr	40	00ff ffff	[EXT]		[EXT]					
NEGX.W	Dn	40	4 0ddd								
NEGX.W	dadr	40	01ff ffff	[EXT]		[EXT]					
NEGX.L	Dn	40	8 0ddd								
NEGX.L	dadr	40	10ff ffff	[EXT]		[EXT]					
MOVE	SR,Dn	40	C 0ddd								
MOVE	SR,dadr	40	11ff ffff	[EXT]		[EXT]					
CHK	Dn,dDn	4ddd1	8 0rrr								
CHK	sadr,Dn	4ddd1	10ee eeee	[EXT]		[EXT]					
CHK	data16,Dn	4ddd1	B C	yyyy							
LEA	jadr,An	4ddd1	11jj jjjj	[EXT]		[EXT]					
CLR.B	Dn	42	0 0ddd								
CLR.B	dadr	42	00ff ffff	[EXT]		[EXT]					
CLR.W	Dn	42	4 0ddd								
CLR.W	dadr	42	01ff ffff	[EXT]		[EXT]					
CLR.L	Dn	42	8 0ddd								
CLR.L	dadr	42	10ff ffff	[EXT]		[EXT]					
NEG.B	Dn	44	0 0ddd								
NEG.B	dadr	44	00ff ffff	[EXT]		[EXT]					
NEG.W	Dn	44	4 0ddd								
NEG.W	dadr	44	01ff ffff	[EXT]		[EXT]					
NEG.L	Dn	44	8 0ddd								
NEG.L	dadr	44	10ff ffff	[EXT]		[EXT]					
MOVE	Dn,CCR	44	C 0sss								
MOVE	sadr,CCR	44	11ee eeee	[EXT]		[EXT]					
MOVE	data8,CCR	44	F C	00	yy						
NOT.B	Dn	46	0 0ddd								
NOT.B	dadr	46	00ff ffff	[EXT]		[EXT]					
NOT.W	Dn	46	4 0ddd								
NOT.W	dadr	46	01ff ffff	[EXT]		[EXT]					
NOT.L	Dn	46	8 0ddd								
NOT.L	dadr	46	10ff ffff	[EXT]		[EXT]					
MOVE	Dn,SR	46	C 0sss								
MOVE	sadr,SR	46	11ee eeee	[EXT]		[EXT]					
MOVE	data16,SR	46	F C	yyyy							
NBCD	Dn	48	0 0ddd								
NBCD	dadr	48	00ff ffff	[EXT]		[EXT]					
SWAP	Dn	48	4 0rrr								
PEA	jadr	48	01jj jjjj	[EXT]		[EXT]					
EXT.W	Dn	48	8 0ddd								
MOVEM.W	reg-list,madr	48	10hh hhhh	mmmm		[EXT]		[EXT]			
MOVEM.W	reg-list,-(An)	48	A 0ddd	kkkk							
EXT.L	Dn	48	C 0ddd								
MOVEM.L	reg-list,madr	48	11hh hhhh	mmmm		[EXT]		[EXT]			
MOVE.L	reg-list,-(An)	48	E 0ddd	kkkk							
TST.B	Dn	4A	0 0rrr								
TST.B	dadr	4A	00ff ffff	[EXT]		[EXT]					
TST.W	Dn	4A	4 0rrr								
TST.W	dadr	4A	01ff ffff	[EXT]		[EXT]					
TST.L	Dn	4A	8 0rrr								
TST.L	dadr	4A	10ff ffff	[EXT]		[EXT]					
TAS	Dn	4A	C 0rrr								
TAS	dadr	4A	11ff ffff	[EXT]		[EXT]					
MOVEM.W	jadr,reg-list	4C	10jj jjjj	mmmm		[EXT]		[EXT]			
MOVEM.W	(An)+,reg-list	4C	A 0sss	mmmm							
MOVEM.L	(An)+,reg-list	4C	E 0sss	mmmm							
MOVEM.L	jadr,reg-list	4C	11jj jjjj	mmmm		[EXT]		[EXT]			
MOVEM.L	(An)+,reg-list	4C	E 0sss	mmmm							
TRAP	vector	4E	4 vvvv								

Table B-2. MC68000 Object Codes in Numerical Order (Continued)

Instruction		Byte 1	Byte 2	Byte 3	Byte 4	Byte 5
LINK	An,d16	4E	5 0rrr	xxxx		
UNLK	An	4E	5 1rrr			
MOVE	An,USP	4E	6 0sss			
MOVE	USP,An	4E	6 1sss			
RESET		4E	7 0			
NOP		4E	7 1			
STOP	data16	4E	7 2	yyyy		
RTE		4E	7 3			
RTS		4E	7 5			
TRAPV		4E	7 6			
RTR		4E	7 7			
JSR	jadr	4E	10jj jjjj	[EXT]		[EXT]
JMP	jadr	4E	11jj jjjj	[EXT]		[EXT]
ADDQ.B	data3,Dn	5 bbb0	0 0ddd			
ADDQ.B	data3,dadr	5 bbb0	00ff ffff	[EXT]		[EXT]
ADDQ.W	data3,Dn	5 bbb0	4 0ddd			
ADDQ.W	data3,An	5 bbb0	4 1ddd			
ADDQ.W	data3,dadr	5 bbb0	01ff ffff	[EXT]		[EXT]
ADDQ.L	data3,Dn	5 bbb0	8 0ddd			
ADDQ.L	data3,An	5 bbb0	8 1ddd			
ADDQ.L	data3,dadr	5 bbb0	01ff ffff	[EXT]		[EXT]
ST	Dn	50	C 0ddd			
DBT	Dn,label	50	C 1rrr	xxxx		
ST	dadr	50	11ff ffff	[EXT]		[EXT]
SUBQ.B	data3,Dn	5 bbb1	0 0ddd			
SUBQ.B	data3,dadr	5 bbb1	00ff ffff	[EXT]		[EXT]
SUBQ.W	data3,Dn	5 bbb1	4 0ddd			
SUBQ.W	data3,An	5 bbb1	4 1ddd			
SUBQ.W	data3,dadr	5 bbb1	01ff ffff	[EXT]		[EXT]
SUBQ.L	data3,Dn	5 bbb1	8 0ddd			
SUBQ.L	data3,An	5 bbb1	8 1ddd			
SUBQ.L	data3,dadr	5 bbb1	01ff ffff	[EXT]		[EXT]
SF	Dn	51	C 0ddd			
DBF	Dn,label	51	C 1rrrr	xxxx		
SF	dadr	51	11ff ffff	[EXT]		[EXT]
SHI	Dn	52	C 0ddd			
DBHI	Dn,label	52	C 1rrr	xxxx		
SHI	dadr	52	11ff ffff	[EXT]		[EXT]
SLS	Dn	53	C 0ddd			
DBLS	Dn,label	53	C 1rrr	xxxx		
SLS	dadr	53	11ff ffff	[EXT]		[EXT]
SCC	Dn	54	C 0ddd			
DBCC	Dn,label	54	D 1rrr	xxxx		
SCC	dadr	54	11ff ffff	[EXT]		[EXT]
SCS	Dn	55	C 0ddd			
DBCS	Dn,label	55	C 1rrr	xxxx		
SCS	dadr	55	11ff ffff	[EXT]		[EXT]
SNE	Dn	56	C 0ddd			
DBNE	Dn,label	56	C 1rrr	xxxx		
SNE	dadr	56	11ff ffff	[EXT]		[EXT]
SEQ	Dn	57	C 0ddd			
DBEQ	Dn,label	57	C 1rrrr	xxxx		
SEQ	dadr	57	11ff ffff	[EXT]		[EXT]
SVC	Dn	58	C 0ddd			
DVC	Dn,label	58	C 1rrr	xxxx		
SVC	dadr	58	11ff ffff	[EXT]		[EXT]
SVS	Dn	59	C 0ddd			
DVS	Dn,label	59	C 1rrr	xxxx		
SVS	dadr	59	11ff ffff	[EXT]		[EXT]
SPL	Dn	5A	C 0ddd			
DBPL	Dn,label	5A	C 1rrr	xxxx		
SPL	dadr	5A	11ff ffff	[EXT]		[EXT]
SMI	Dn	5B	C 0ddd			
DBMI	Dn,label	5B	C 1rrr	xxxx		
SMI	dadr	5B	11ff ffff	[EXT]		[EXT]
SGE	Dn	5C	C 0ddd			
DBGE	Dn,label	5C	C 1rrr	xxxx		
SGE	dadr	5C	11ff ffff	[EXT]		[EXT]
SLT	Dn	5D	C 0ddd			
DBLT	Dn,label	5D	C 1rrr	xxxx		
SLT	dadr	5D	11ff ffff	[EXT]		[EXT]
SGT	Dn	5E	C 0ddd			
DBGT	Dn,label	5E	C 1rrr	xxxx		

Table B-2. MC68000 Object Codes in Numerical Order (Continued)

Instruction		Byte 1	Byte 2	Byte 3	Byte 4	Byte 5
SGT	dadr	5E	11ff ffff	[EXT]		[EXT]
SLE	Dn	5F	C Oddd			
DBLE	Dn,label	5F	C 1rrr	xxxx		
SLE	dadr	5F	11ff ffff	[EXT]		[EXT]
BRA	label	60	0 0	xxxx		
BRA	label	60	xx			
BSR	label	61	00	xxxx		
BSR	label	61	xx			
BHI	label	62	00	xxxx		
BHI	label	62	xx			
BLS	label	63	00	xxxx		
BLS	label	63	xx			
BCC	label	64	00	xxxx		
BCC	label	64	xx			
BCS	label	65	00	xxxx		
BCS	label	65	xx			
BNE	label	66	00	xxxx		
BNE	label	66	xx			
BEQ	label	67	00	xxxx		
BEQ	label	67	xx			
BVC	label	68	00	xxxx		
BVC	label	68	xx			
BVS	label	69	00	xxxx		
BVS	label	69	xx			
BPL	label	6A	00	xxxx		
BPL	label	6A	xx			
BMI	label	6B	00	xxxx		
BMI	label	6B	xx			
BGE	label	6C	00	xxxx		
BGE	label	6C	xx			
BLT	label	6D	00	xxxx		
BLT	label	6D	xx			
BGT	label	6E	00	xxxx		
BGT	label	6E	xx			
BLE	label	6F	00	xxxx		
BLE	label	6F	xx			
MOVEQ	data8,Dn	7ddd0	yy			
OR. B	sDn,dDn	8ddd0	0 Osss			
OR. B	sadr,Dn	8ddd0	00ee aeee	[EXT]		[EXT]
OR. W	sDn,dDn	8ddd0	4 Osss			
OR.W	sadr,Dn	8ddd0	01eeeeee	[EXT]		[EXT]
OR.L	sDn,dDn	8ddd0	8 Osss			
OR.L	sadr,Dn	8ddd0	10eeeeee	[EXT]		[EXT]
DIVU	sDn,dDn	8ddd0	C Osss			
DIVU	sadr,Dn	8ddd0	11eeeeee	[EXT]		[EXT]
DIVU	data16,Dn	8ddd0	F C	yyyy		
SBC	sDn,dDn	8ddd1	0 Osss			
SBCD	−(sAn),−(dAn)	8ddd1	0 1sss			
OR.B	Dn,dadr	8sss1	00ff ffff	[EXT]		[EXT]
OR.W	Dn,dadr	8sss1	01ff ffff	[EXT]		[EXT]
OR.L	Dn,dadr	8sss1	10ff ffff	[EXT]		[EXT]
DIVS	sDn,dDn	8ddd1	C Osss			
DIVS	sadr,Dn	8ddd1	11ee eeee	[EXT]		[EXT]
DIVS	data16,Dn	8ddd1	F C	yyyy		
SUB.B	sDn,dDn	9ddd0	0 Osss			
SUB.B	sadr,Dn	9ddd0	00ee eeee	[EXT]		[EXT]
SUB.W	rs,Dn	9ddd0	4 tsss			
SUB.W	sadr,Dn	9ddd0	01ee eeee	[EXT]		[EXT]
SUB.L	rs,Dn	9ddd0	8 tsss			
SUB.L	sadr,Dn	9ddd0	10eeeeee	[EXT]		[EXT]
SUB.W	rs,An	9ddd0	C tsss			
SUB.W	sadr,An	9ddd0	11eeeeee	[EXT]		[EXT]
SUB.W	data16,An	9ddd0	F C	yyyy		
SUBX.B	sDn,dDn	9ddd1	0 Osss			
SUBX.B	−(sAn),−(dAn)	9ddd1	0 1sss			
SUB.B	Dn,dadr	9sss1	00ffffff	[EXT]		[EXT]
SUBX.W	sDn,dDn	9ddd1	4 Osss			
SUBX.W	−(sAn),−(dAn)	9ddd1	4 1sss			
SUB.W	Dn,dadr	9sss1	01ff ffff	[EXT]		[EXT]
SUBX.L	sDn,dDn	9ddd1	8 Osss			
SUBX.L	−(sAn),−(dAn)	9ddd1	8 1sss			
SUB.L	Dn,dadr	9sss1	10ffffff	[EXT]		[EXT]
SUB.L	rs,An	9ddd1	C tsss			

Table B-2. MC68000 Object Codes in Numerical Order (Continued)

Instruction	Byte 1	Byte 2	Byte 3	Byte 4	Byte 5	Byte 6	Byte 7	Byte 8	Byte 9	Byte 10
SUB.L sadr,An	9 ddd1	11eeeeee	[EXT]		[EXT]					
SUB.L data32,An	9 ddd1	F C	yyyy		zzzz					
CMP.B sDn,dDn	B ddd0	0 0sss								
CMP.B sadr,Dn	B ddd0	00eeeeee	[EXT]		[EXT]					
CMP.W rs,Dn	B ddd0	4 tsss								
CMP.W sadr,Dn	B ddd0	01eeeeee	[EXT]		[EXT]					
CMP.L rs,Dn	B ddd0	8 tsss								
CMP.L sadr,Dn	B ddd0	10eeeeee	[EXT]		[EXT]					
CMP.W rs,An	B ddd0	C tsss								
CMP.W sadr,An	B ddd0	11eeeeee	[EXT]		[EXT]					
CMP.W data16,An	B ddd0	F C	yyyy							
EOR.B sDn,dDn	B sss1	0 0ddd								
CMPM.B (sAn)+,(dAn)+	B ddd1	0 1sss								
EOR.B Dn,dadr	B sss1	00ffffff	[EXT]		[EXT]					
EOR.W sDn,dDn	B sss1	4 0ddd								
CMPM.W (sAn)+,(dAn)+	B ddd1	4 1sss								
EOR.W Dn,dadr	B sss1	01ffffff	[EXT]		[EXT]					
EOR.L sDn,dDn	B sss1	8 0ddd								
CMPM.L (sAn)+,(dAn)+	B ddd1	8 1sss								
EOR.L Dn,dadr	B sss1	10ffffff	[EXT]		[EXT]					
CMP.L rs,An	B ddd1	C tsss								
CMP.L sadr,An	B ddd1	11eeeeee	[EXT]		[EXT]					
CMP.L data32,An	B ddd1	F C	yyyy		zzzz					
AND.B sDn,dDn	C ddd0	0 0sss								
AND.B sadr,Dn	C ddd0	00eeeeee	[EXT]		[EXT]					
AND.W sDn,dDn	C ddd0	4 0sss								
AND.W sadr,Dn	C ddd0	01eeeeee	[EXT]		[EXT]					
AND.L sDn,dDn	C ddd0	8 0sss								
AND.L sadr,Dn	C ddd0	10eeeeee	[EXT]		[EXT]					
MULU sDn,dDn	C ddd0	C 0sss								
MULU sadr,Dn	C ddd0	11eeeeee	[EXT]		[EXT]					
MULU data16,Dn	C ddd0	F C	yyyy							
ABCD sDn,dDn	C ddd1	0 0sss								
ABCD -(sAn),-(dAn)	C ddd1	0 1sss								
AND.B Dn,dadr	C sss1	00ffffff	[EXT]		[EXT]					
EXG Dn,Dn	C sss1	4 0ddd								
EXG An,An	C sss1	4 1ddd								
AND.W Dn,dadr	C sss1	01ffffff	[EXT]		[EXT]					
EXG Dn,An or An,Dn	C sss1	8 1ddd								
AND.L Dn,dadr	C sss1	10ffffff	[EXT]		[EXT]					
MULS sDn,dDn	C ddd1	C 0sss								
MULS sadr,Dn	C ddd1	11eeeeee	[EXT]		[EXT]					
MULS data16,Dn	C ddd1	F C	yyyy							
ADD.B sDn,dDn	D ddd0	0 0sss								
ADD.B sadr,Dn	D dddC	00eeeeee	[EXT]		[EXT]					
ADD.W rs,Dn	D ddd0	4 tsss								
ADD.W sadr,Dn	D ddd0	01eeeeee	[EXT]		[EXT]					
ADD.L rs,Dn	D ddd0	8 tsss								
ADD.L sadr,Dn	D ddd0	10eeeeee	[EXT]		[EXT]					
ADD.W rs,An	D ddd0	C tsss								
ADD.W sadr,An	D ddd0	11eeeeee	[EXT]		[EXT]					
ADD.W data16,An	D ddd0	F C	yyyy							
ADDX.B sDn,dDn	D ddd1	0 0sss								
ADDX.B -(sAn),-(dAn)	D ddd1	0 1sss								
ADD.B Dn,dadr	D sss1	00ffffff	[EXT]		[EXT]					
ADDX.W sDn,dDn	D ddd1	4 0sss								
ADDX.W -(sAn),-(dAn)	D ddd1	4 1sss								
ADD.W Dn,dadr	D sss1	01ffffff	[EXT]		[EXT]					
ADDX.L sDn,dDn	D ddd1	8 0sss								
ADDX.L -(sAn),-(dAn)	D ddd1	8 1sss								
ADD.L Dn,dadr	D sss1	10ffffff	[EXT]		[EXT]					
ADD.L rs,An	D ddd1	C tsss								
ADD.L sadr,An	D ddd1	11eeeeee	[EXT]		[EXT]					
ADD.L data32,An	D ddd1	F C	yyyy		zzzz					
ASR.B count,Dn	E ccc0	0 0ddd								
LSR.B count,Dn	E ccc0	0 1ddd								
ROXR.B count,Dn	E ccc0	1 0ddd								
ROR.B count,Dn	E ccc0	1 1ddd								
ASR.B Dn,dDn	E rrr0	2 0ddd								
LSR.B Dn,dDn	E rrr0	2 1ddd								
ROXR.B Dn,dDn	E rrr0	3 0ddd								
ROR.B Dn,dDn	E rrr0	3 1ddd								

Table B-2. MC68000 Object Codes in Numerical Order (Continued)

Instruction		Byte 1	Byte 2	Byte 3	Byte 4	Byte 5	Byte 6	Byte 7	Byte 8	Byte 9	Byte 10
ASR.W	count,Dn	E ccc0 4	0ddd								
LSR.W	count,Dn	E ccc0 4	1ddd								
ROXR.W	count,Dn	E ccc0 5	0ddd								
ROR.W	count,Dn	E ccc0 5	1ddd								
ASR.W	Dn,dDn	E rrr0 6	0ddd								
LSR.W	Dn,dDn	E rrr0 6	1ddd								
ROXR.W	Dn,dDn	E rrr0 7	0ddd								
ROR.W	Dn,dDn	E rrr0 7	1ddd								
ASR.L	count,Dn	E ccc0 8	0ddd								
LSR.L	count,Dn	E ccc0 8	1ddd								
ROXR.L	count,Dn	E ccc0 9	0ddd								
ROR.L	count, Dn	E ccc0 9	1ddd								
ASR.L	Dn,dDn	E rrr0 A	0ddd								
LSR.L	Dn,dDn	E rrr0 A	1ddd								
ROXR.L	Dn,dDn	E rrr0 B	0ddd								
ROR.L	Dn,dDn	E rrr0 B	1ddd								
ASR	dadr	E 0	11ffffff	[EXT]		[EXT]					
ASL.B	count,Dn	E ccc1 0	0ddd								
LSL.B	count,Dn	E ccc1 0	1ddd								
ROXL.B	count,Dn	E ccc1 1	0ddd								
ROL.B	count,Dn	E ccc1 1	1ddd								
ASL.B	Dn,dDn	E rrr1 2	0ddd								
LSL.B	Dn,dDn	E rrr1 2	1ddd								
ROXL.B	Dn,dDn	E rrr1 3	0ddd								
ROL.B	Dn,dDn	E rrr1 3	1ddd								
ASL.W	count,Dn	E ccc1 4	0ddd								
LSL.W	count,Dn	E ccc1 4	1ddd								
ROXL.W	count,Dn	E ccc1 5	0ddd								
ROL.W	count,Dn	E ccc1 5	1ddd								
ASL.W	Dn,dDn	E rrr1 6	0ddd								
LSL.W	Dn,dDn	E rrr1 6	1ddd								
ROXL.W	Dn,dDn	E rrr1 7	0ddd								
ROL.W	Dn,dDn	E rrr1 7	1ddd								
ASL.L	count,Dn	E ccc1 8	0ddd								
LSL.L	count,Dn	E ccc1 8	1ddd								
ROXL.L	count,Dn	E ccc1 9	0ddd								
ROL.L	count,Dn	E ccc1 9	1ddd								
ASL.L	Dn,dDn	E rrr1 A	0ddd								
LSL.L	Dn,dDn	E rrr1 A	1ddd								
ROXL.L	Dn,dDn	E rrr1 B	0ddd								
ROL.L	Dn,dDn	E rrr1 B	1ddd								
ASL	dadr	E 1	11ffffff	[EXT]		[EXT]					
LSR	dadr	E 2	11ffffff	[EXT]		[EXT]					
LSL	dadr	E 3	11ffffff	[EXT]		[EXT]					
ROXR	dadr	E 4	11ffffff	[EXT]		[EXT]					
ROXL	dadr	E 5	11ffffff	[EXT]		[EXT]					
ROR	dadr	E 6	11ffffff	[EXT]		[EXT]					
ROL	dadr	E 7	11ffffff	[EXT]		[EXT]					

C
Data Sheets

This appendix contains specific electrical and timing data for the MC68000L4, MC68000L6 and MC68000L. The waveforms provided here should only be referenced in regard to the edge-to-edge measurement of the timing specifications. They are not intended as a functional description of the input and output signals. Refer to Chapters 3, 4, and 7 for descriptions and illustrations of device operation.

MC68000L4/MC68000L6/MC68000L

AC ELECTRICAL SPECIFICATIONS (V_{CC} = 5.0 Vdc ± 5%; V_{SS} = 0 Vdc; T_A = 0°C to 70°C)

Number	Characteristic	Symbol	4 MHz MC68000L4 Min	4 MHz MC68000L4 Max	6 MHz MC68000L6 Min	6 MHz MC68000L6 Max	8 MHz MC68000L Min	8 MHz MC68000L Max	Unit
1	Clock Period	t_{cyc}	250	500	167	500	125	500	ns
2	Clock Width Low	t_{CL}	115	250	75	250	55	250	ns
3	Clock Width High	t_{CH}	115	250	75	250	55	250	ns
4	Clock Fall Time	t_{Cf}	–	10	–	10	–	10	ns
5	Clock Rise Time	t_{Cr}	–	10	–	10	–	10	ns
6	Clock Low to Address/FC Valid	t_{CLAV}	–	90	–	80	–	70	ns
7	Clock High to Address/FC/Data High Impedance (maximum)	t_{CHAZx}	–	120	–	100	–	80	ns
8	Clock High to Address/FC Invalid (minimum)	t_{CHAZn}	20	–	20	–	20	–	ns
9[1]	Clock High to $\overline{AS}$, $\overline{DS}$ Low (maximum)	t_{CHSLx}	–	80	–	70	–	60	ns
10	Clock High to $\overline{AS}$, $\overline{DS}$ Low (minimum)	t_{CHSLn}	20	–	20	–	20	–	ns
11[2]	Address/FC Valid to $\overline{AS}$, $\overline{DS}$ (read) Low	t_{AVSL}	55	–	35	–	30	–	ns
12[1]	Clock Low to $\overline{AS}$, $\overline{DS}$ High	t_{CLSH}	–	90	–	80	–	70	ns
13[2]	$\overline{AS}$, $\overline{DS}$ High to Address/FC Invalid	t_{SHAZ}	60	–	40	–	30	–	ns
14[2]	$\overline{AS}$, $\overline{DS}$ Width Low	t_{SL}	285	–	170	–	115	–	ns
15[2]	$\overline{AS}$, $\overline{DS}$ Width High	t_{SH}	285	–	180	–	150	–	ns
16	Clock High to $\overline{AS}$, $\overline{DS}$ High Impedance	t_{CHSZ}	–	120	–	100	–	80	ns
17[2]	$\overline{DS}$ High to R/$\overline{W}$ High	t_{SHRH}	60	–	50	–	40	–	ns
18[1]	Clock High to R/$\overline{W}$ High (maximum)	t_{CHRHx}	–	90	–	80	–	70	ns
19	Clock High to R/$\overline{W}$ High (minimum)	t_{CHRHn}	20	–	20	–	20	–	ns
20[1]	Clock High to R/$\overline{W}$ Low	t_{CHRL}	–	90	–	80	–	70	ns
21[2]	Address/FC Valid to R/$\overline{W}$ Low	t_{AVRL}	45	–	25	–	20	–	ns
22[2]	R/$\overline{W}$ Low to $\overline{DS}$ Low (write)	t_{RLSL}	200	–	140	–	80	–	ns
23	Clock Low to Data Out Valid	t_{CLDO}	–	90	–	80	–	70	ns
24	Clock High to R/$\overline{W}$, $\overline{VMA}$ High Impedance	t_{CHRZ}	–	120	–	100	–	80	ns
25[2]	$\overline{DS}$ High to Data Out Invalid	t_{SHDO}	60	–	40	–	30	–	ns
26[2]	Data Out Valid to $\overline{DS}$ Low (write)	t_{DOSL}	55	–	35	–	30	–	ns
27	Data In to Clock Low (set up time)	t_{DICL}	30	–	25	–	15	–	ns
28[2]	$\overline{DS}$ High to $\overline{DTACK}$ High	t_{SHDAH}	0	240	0	160	0	120	ns
29	$\overline{DS}$ High to Data Invalid (hold time)	t_{SHDI}	0	–	0	–	0	–	ns
30	$\overline{AS}$, $\overline{DS}$ High to $\overline{BERR}$ High	t_{SHBEH}	0	–	0	–	0	–	ns
31[2]	$\overline{DTACK}$ Low to Data In (setup time)	t_{DALDI}	–	180	–	120	–	90	ns
32	$\overline{HALT}$ and $\overline{RESET}$ Input Transition Time	t_{RHrf}	0	200	0	200	0	200	ns
33	Clock High to $\overline{BG}$ Low	t_{CHGL}	–	90	–	80	–	70	ns
34	Clock High to $\overline{BG}$ High	t_{CHGH}	–	90	–	80	–	70	ns
35	$\overline{BR}$ Low to $\overline{BG}$ Low	t_{BRLGL}	1.5	3.0	1.5	3.0	1.5	3.0	clk. per.
36	$\overline{BR}$ High to $\overline{BG}$ High	t_{BRHGH}	1.5	3.0	1.5	3.0	1.5	3.0	clk. per.
37	$\overline{BGACK}$ Low to $\overline{BG}$ High	t_{GALGH}	1.5	3.0	1.5	3.0	1.5	3.0	clk. per.
38	$\overline{BG}$ Low to Bus High Impedance (with $\overline{AS}$ high)	t_{GLZ}	0	1.5	0	1.5	0	1.5	clk. per.
39	$\overline{BG}$ Width High	t_{GH}	1.5	–	1.5	–	1.5	–	clk. per.
40	Clock Low to $\overline{VMA}$ Low	t_{CLVML}	–	90	–	80	–	70	ns
41	Clock Low to E Transition	t_{CLE}	–	65	–	60	–	55	ns
42	E Output Rise and Fall Time	t_{Erf}	–	25	–	25	–	25	ns
43[2]	$\overline{VMA}$ Low to E High	t_{VMLEH}	325	–	240	–	200	–	ns
44	$\overline{AS}$, $\overline{DS}$ High to $\overline{VPA}$ High	t_{SHVPH}	0	240	0	160	0	120	ns
45	E Low to Address/$\overline{VMA}$/FC Invalid	t_{ELAI}	50	–	35	–	30	–	ns
46	$\overline{BGACK}$ Width	t_{BGL}	1.5	–	1.5	–	1.5	–	clk. per.
47	Asynchronous Input Setup Time	t_{ASI}	30	–	25	–	20	–	ns
48	$\overline{BERR}$ Low to $\overline{DTACK}$ Low	t_{BELDAL}	50	–	50	–	50	–	ns
49	E Low to $\overline{AS}$, $\overline{DS}$ Invalid	t_{ELSI}	–80	–	–80	–	–80	–	ns
50	E Width High	t_{EH}	900	–	600	–	450	–	ns
51	E Width Low	t_{EL}	1400	–	900	–	700	–	ns

NOTE 1: For a loading capacitance of less than or equal to 50 pico-farads, subtract 5 nanoseconds from the values given in these columns.

NOTE: 2 Actual value depends on actual clock period.

Data Sheets on pages 110 through 113 reprinted by permission of Motorola Semiconductor Products, Inc.

MC68000L4/MC68000L6/MC68000L

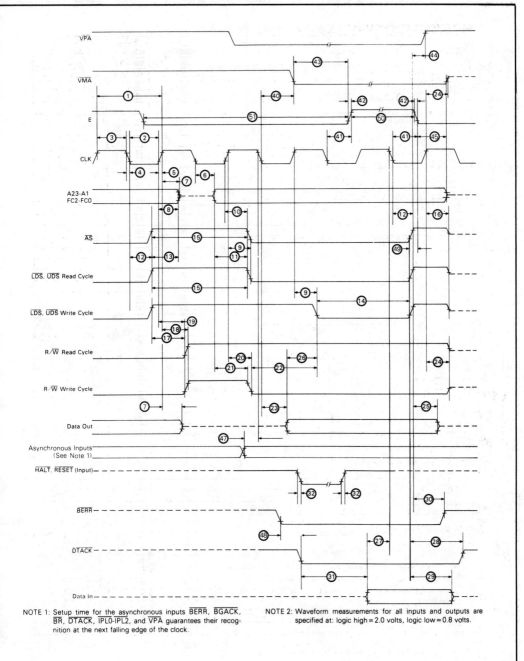

NOTE 1: Setup time for the asynchronous inputs BERR, BGACK, BR, DTACK, IPL0-IPL2, and VPA guarantees their recognition at the next falling edge of the clock.

NOTE 2: Waveform measurements for all inputs and outputs are specified at: logic high = 2.0 volts, logic low = 0.8 volts.

MC68000L4/MC68000L6/MC68000L

ELECTRICAL CHARACTERISTICS ($V_{CC} = 5.0$ Vdc $\pm 5\%$; $V_{SS} = 0$ Vdc; T_A 0°C to 70°C, Figures 33, 34, 35)

Characteristic		Symbol	Min	Typ	Max	Unit
Input High Voltage		V_{IH}	2.0	–	V_{CC}	Vdc
Input Low Voltage		V_{IL}	$V_{SS} - 0.3$	–	0.8	Vdc
Input Leakage Current	$\overline{BERR}$, $\overline{BGACK}$, $\overline{BR}$, $\overline{DTACK}$, $\overline{IPL0}$-$\overline{IPL2}$, $\overline{VPA}$	I_{in}	–	1.0	–	μAdc
	$\overline{HALT}$, $\overline{RESET}$		–	2.0	–	
Three-State (Off State) Input Current	$\overline{AS}$, A1-A23, D0-D15 FC0-FC2, $\overline{LDS}$, R/$\overline{W}$, $\overline{UDS}$, $\overline{VMA}$	I_{TSI}	–	7.0	–	μAdc
Output High Voltage ($I_{OH} = -400$ μAdc)	$\overline{AS}$, A1-A23, $\overline{BG}$, D0-D15, E, FC0-FC2, $\overline{LDS}$, R/$\overline{W}$, $\overline{UDS}$, $\overline{VMA}$	V_{OH}	2.4	–	–	Vdc
Output Low Voltage						
($I_{OL} = 1.6$ mA)	$\overline{HALT}$		–	–	0.5	
($I_{OL} = 3.2$ mA)	A1-A23, $\overline{BG}$, E, FC0-FC2	V_{OL}	–	–	0.5	Vdc
($I_{OL} = 5.0$ mA)	$\overline{RESET}$		–	–	0.5	
($I_{OL} = 5.3$ mA)	$\overline{AS}$, D0-D15, $\overline{LDS}$, R/$\overline{W}$, $\overline{UDS}$, $\overline{VMA}$		–	–	0.5	
Power Dissipation (Clock Frequency = 8 MHz)		P_D	–	1.0	–	W
Capacitance (Package Type Dependent) ($V_{in} = 0$ Vdc; $T_A = 25$°C; Frequency = 1 MHz)		C_{in}	–	10.0	–	pF

FIGURE 33 — RESET TEST LOAD

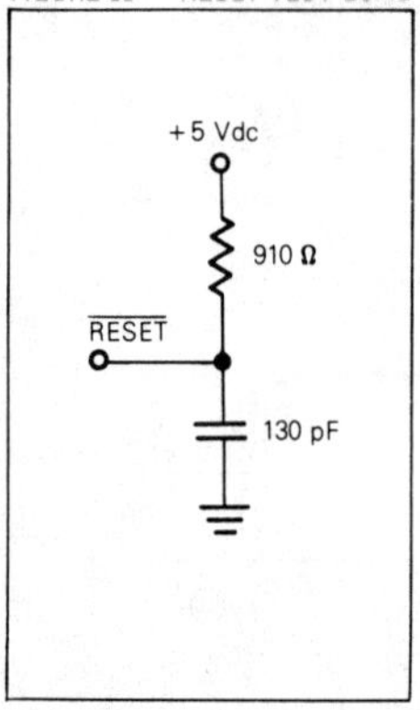

+5 Vdc

910 Ω

$\overline{RESET}$

130 pF

FIGURE 34 — HALT TEST LOAD

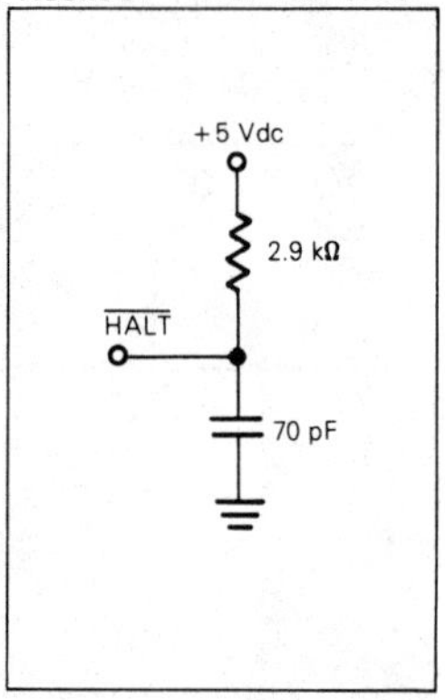

+5 Vdc

2.9 kΩ

$\overline{HALT}$

70 pF

FIGURE 35 — TEST LOADS

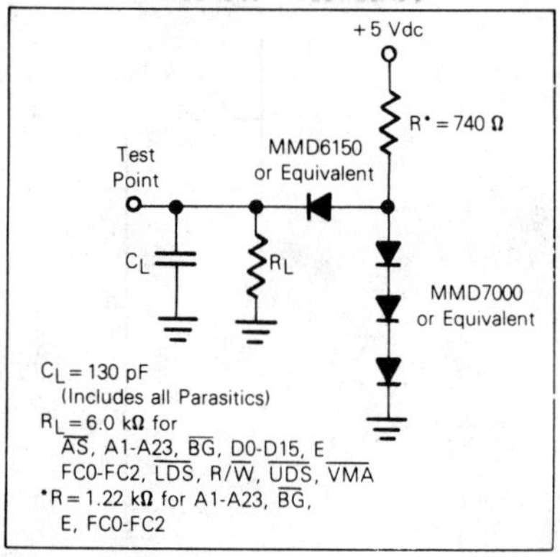

+5 Vdc

R* = 740 Ω

Test Point

MMD6150 or Equivalent

C_L R_L

MMD7000 or Equivalent

$C_L = 130$ pF
(Includes all Parasitics)
$R_L = 6.0$ kΩ for
$\overline{AS}$, A1-A23, $\overline{BG}$, D0-D15, E
FC0-FC2, $\overline{LDS}$, R/$\overline{W}$, $\overline{UDS}$, $\overline{VMA}$
*R = 1.22 kΩ for A1-A23, $\overline{BG}$,
E, FC0-FC2

FIGURE 36 — INPUT CLOCK WAVEFORM

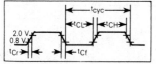

2.0 V
0.8 V
t_{Cr} t_{Cf}
t_{cyc} t_{CL} t_{CH}

MAXIMUM RATINGS

Rating	Symbol	Value	Unit
Supply Voltage	V_{CC}	–0.3 to +7.0	Vdc
Input Voltage	V_{in}	–0.3 to +7.0	Vdc
Operating Temperature Range	T_A	0 to 70	°C
Storage Temperature	T_{stg}	–55 to 150	°C

CLOCK TIMING (Figure 36)

Characteristic	Symbol	4 MHz MC6800L4		6 MHz MC68000L6		8 MHz MC68000L		Unit
		Min	Max	Min	Max	Min	Max	Unit
Frequency of Operation	F	2.0	4.0	2.0	6.0	2.0	8.0	MHz
Cycle Time	t_{cyc}	250	500	167	500	125	500	ns
Clock Pulse Width	t_{CL} t_{CH}	115 115	250 250	75 75	250 250	55 55	250 250	ns
Rise and Fall Times	t_{Cr} t_{Cf}	– –	10 10	– –	10 10	– –	10 10	ns

MC68000L4/MC68000L6/MC68000L

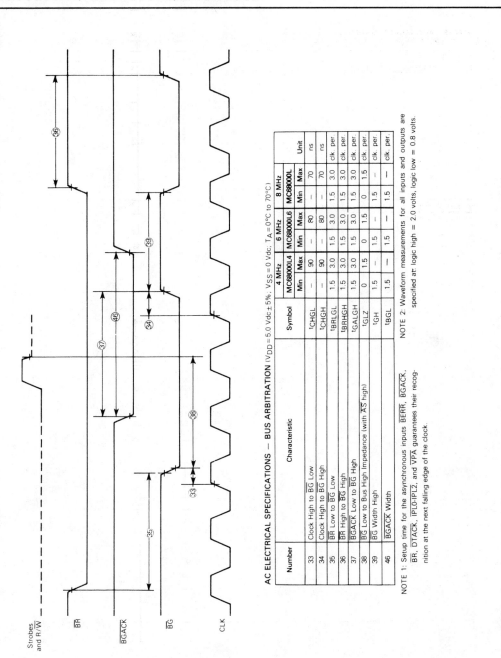

AC ELECTRICAL SPECIFICATIONS — BUS ARBITRATION (V_{DD}=5.0 Vdc±5%; V_{SS}=0 Vdc; T_A=0°C to 70°C)

Number	Characteristic	Symbol	4 MHz MC68000L4		6 MHz MC68000L6		8 MHz MC68000L		Unit
			Min	Max	Min	Max	Min	Max	
33	Clock High to $\overline{BG}$ Low	tCHGL	—	90	—	80	—	70	ns
34	Clock High to $\overline{BG}$ High	tCHGH	—	90	—	80	—	70	ns
35	$\overline{BR}$ Low to $\overline{BG}$ Low	tBRLGL	1.5	3.0	1.5	3.0	1.5	3.0	clk. per.
36	$\overline{BR}$ High to $\overline{BG}$ High	tBRHGH	1.5	3.0	1.5	3.0	1.5	3.0	clk. per.
37	$\overline{BGACK}$ Low to $\overline{BG}$ High	tGALGH	1.5	3.0	1.5	3.0	1.5	3.0	clk. per.
38	$\overline{BG}$ Low to Bus High Impedance (with $\overline{AS}$ high)	tGLZ	0	1.5	0	1.5	0	1.5	clk. per.
39	$\overline{BG}$ Width High	tGH	1.5	—	1.5	—	1.5	—	clk. per.
46	$\overline{BGACK}$ Width	tBGL	1.5	—	1.5	—	1.5	—	clk. per.

NOTE 1: Setup time for the asynchronous inputs $\overline{BERR}$, $\overline{BGACK}$, $\overline{BR}$, $\overline{DTACK}$, $\overline{IPL0}$-$\overline{IPL2}$, and $\overline{VPA}$ guarantees their recognition at the next falling edge of the clock.

NOTE 2: Waveform measurements for all inputs and outputs are specified at: logic high = 2.0 volts, logic low = 0.8 volts.

Strobes and R/$\overline{W}$

$\overline{BR}$

$\overline{BGACK}$

$\overline{BG}$

CLK

Index

OSBORNE/McGraw-Hill Books of Interest

The 8086 Book
by R. Rector and G. Alexy
8080 Programming for Logic Design
by Adam Osborne
6800 Programming for Logic Design
by Adam Osborne
Z80 Programming for Logic Design
by Adam Osborne

8080A/8085 Assembly Language Programming
by L. Leventhal
6800 Assembly Language Programming
by L. Leventhal
Z80 Assembly Language Programming
by L. Leventhal
6502 Assembly Language Programming
by L. Leventhal
Z8000 Assembly Language Programming
by L. Leventhal et al.
Running Wild: The Next Industrial Revolution
by Adam Osborne
PET/CBM Personal Computer Guide — Second Edition
by Adam Osborne and Carroll Donahue
PET and the IEEE 488 Bus (GPIB)
by E. Fisher and C. W. Jensen
Practical Basic Programs
by L. Poole et al.
Some Common BASIC Programs
by L. Poole and M. Borchers
Payroll with Cost Accounting — CBASIC
by Lon Poole et al.
Accounts Payable and Accounts Receivable — CBASIC
by Lon Poole et al.
General Ledger — CBASIC
by Lon Poole et al.
Some Common Basic Programs — PET/CBM
edited by Lon Poole et al.